THE INSPIRATIONAL

Speaker's

RESOURCE

Tools for Reaching Your Audience Every Time

STAN TOLER

BEACON HILL PRESS
OF KANSAS CITY

Copyright 2009
by Stan Toler and Beacon Hill Press of Kansas City

ISBN 978-0-8341-2449-3

Printed in the
United States of America

Cover Design: J.R. Caines
Interior Design: Sharon Page

Library of Congress Cataloging-in-Publication Data

Toler, Stan.
    The inspirational speaker's resource : tools for reaching your audience every time / Stan Toler.
        p. cm.
    Includes bibliographical references.
    ISBN 978-0-8341-2449-3 (pbk.)
    1. Public speaking. 2. Public speaking—Religious aspects—Christianity.
I. Title.

    PN4121.T65 2009
    808.5′1—dc22

2009012815

10 9 8 7 6 5 4 3 2 1

PUBLIC SPEAKING

Public speaking is the process of speaking to a group of people in a structured, deliberate manner intended to inform, influence, or entertain the listeners. . . . In public speaking, as in any form of communication, there are five basic elements, often expressed as *"who* is saying *what* to *whom* using what *medium* with what *effects*?"* The purpose of public speaking can range from simply transmitting information, to motivating people to act, to simply telling a story.[1]

CONTENTS

FOREWORD

Dr. Stan Toler is a great friend of Beacon Hill Press. In fact, Beacon Hill has had the privilege of serving as Stan's publisher for more than 30 years. His first title, *Essentials in Evangelism*, was released in 1979. Stan was 28 years old. *Essentials of Evangelism* sold more than 20,000 copies, a great success by any measure. This debut title was the beginning of a long and fruitful partnership between writer and publisher.

The Inspirational Speaker's Resource is Stan's 71st book. In my view, it may be one of his most important. Dr. John Maxwell calls Stan a "pastor to America's pastors." Stan has invested his life in the higher calling of mentoring and training pastors, equipping them to become shepherds who model servanthood and excellence in leadership to their local faith communities. "Anyone can be a pastor; it takes an extraordinary commitment to become a shepherd," Stan says. He should know. His shepherding journey took him through Florida, Ohio, and Tennessee before he settled in Oklahoma, where he has spent the last 25 years building Trinity Church of the Nazarene from a congregation of 300 to more than 1000 persons.

During his tenure at Trinity, Stan has continued to invest in a legacy of pastoral health. Mid-America Christian University established the Stan Toler Leadership Institute, which is specifically created to equip and train pastoral students. To date, more than 69,000 students have been touched through the Institute, which is getting ready to expand to other campuses.

A significant part of Stan's equipping regimen is training leaders to be excellent communicators and pulpiteers. "There is no substitute for good preaching and teaching," Stan says. "Effective communication is essential for success in every area of life. Leaders can not afford to be poor communicators."

Stan knows this firsthand. He has spoken in more than 10,000 settings in his career, and not all of those were in church. Stan takes his message to leaders around the world in corporate settings as well as seminars, conferences, and workshops. More than a million participants have attended Stan's seminars, and sales of his books top the two-million mark.

Professionals know that the ability to communicate publicly is an essential skill for upward mobility within a company setting. In *The Inspirational Speaker's Resource,* Stan gives us all the tools we need to succeed in whatever situation we are in, whether it's a simple demonstration at work or a more formal presentation in front of a large and diverse audience.

In this book, you will find tips on overcoming stage fright (one of the top five fears of people, according to just about any such list you reference), techniques for motivating your audience, and tools for organizing your thoughts. In addition, Stan has included top 10 lists, humorous stories, quotations, and anecdotes to energize and transform your presentations. He doesn't stop there. He also provides practical skills to enhance your public persona, including both verbal and nonverbal communication.

Thank you, Stan, for your generous spirit and your lasting contribution to the ministry of pastors, laypersons, and leaders. They may never meet you in person or have the privilege of shaking your hand, but they have been shaped by your dedication and your care.

Happy 30th anniversary, Stan. Beacon Hill Press is proud to be your publisher.

—Bonnie Perry
Director, Beacon Hill Press of Kansas City

ACKNOWLEDGMENTS

Special thanks to Bonnie Perry, Barry Russell, Richard Buckner, and the entire Beacon Hill team. Thanks also to Deloris Leonard, Jerry Brecheisen, and Pat Diamond for editorial assistance.

INTRODUCTION

"I have a dream."

Just words? Of course not! The combination of letters and words in that phrase from Dr. Martin Luther King Jr.'s history-making speech during the civil rights movement of the 1960s inspired millions. The entire speech was spoken with dynamic energy, focused on the needs of the audience, and delivered with the right technique.

The Greatest Speech

Another speech contained these anointed words, "Blessed are the pure in heart, for they will see God" (Matt. 5:8). They were from the Sermon on the Mount, which tops every speech. They were spoken by a carpenter apprentice who also was the Son of God. They did more than inspire. They brought healing and wholeness and have been the foundation for reform and revival across generations.

Public speaking provides the rare opportunity to change lives, to inspire and heal, to inform and motivate. It is a high calling.

Ten Thousand Sermons Later

I admit it. I am not a man of few words.

For the last three decades I have traveled around the planet in planes, buses, taxis, and rental cars and have spoken to audiences of several or several thousand—in auditoriums, online, and on radio and TV. A while back I tallied up just the number of sermons I had preached, not counting speeches or seminars. The 10,000-sermon total wasn't that surprising. I began speaking from a church platform when I was a teenager—and my sons would say I haven't stopped preaching yet.

Along the way, I've shared platforms and stages with some of the great inspirational and motivational speakers of our time. I've watched them in the moments before they spoke to their waiting audiences. I've taken notes during their delivery. I've asked them about the techniques that have served them so well. I've heard the stories that drove home their beliefs. This book combines the years of listening with the years of speaking. *The Inspirational Speaker's Resource* is both about technique and resources—about *what* to say and *how* to say it.

I write it with a passion to help every public speaker learn some of the valuable lessons I have learned—including how to hack your way out of the dreaded "brush," that painful moment when all of your brilliant thoughts seem to be wrapped in muddled mediocrity and piled next to your briefcase.

Spark in the Soul

Charlie (Tremendous) Jones once said, "I believe the fires of greatness in our hearts can be kept aglow only after we have a sense of urgency."[1] Let's be honest, not everyone will remember your greatest speech, sermon, or seminar presentation! Some will even struggle to remember your name. But that doesn't mean what you say won't leave a spark in their soul. Truth spoken in love will always leave a lasting impression, whether it is minuscule or major. Your job is to fire away—to keep speaking the truth in the best way you know how.

The apostle Paul was a great speaker (you've heard about that sermon on Mars Hill?). But even this giant among the evangelists realized how vulnerable the public speaker can be. He writes to the Christians in Corinth:

> When I came to you, brothers, I did not come with eloquence or superior wisdom as I proclaimed to you the testimony about God. For I resolved to know nothing while I was with you except Jesus Christ and him crucified. I came to you in weakness and fear, and with much trembling. My message and my preaching were not with wise and persuasive words, but with a demonstration of the Spirit's power, so that your faith might not rest on men's wisdom, but on God's power. (1 Cor. 2:1-5)

There it is! Human weakness joined divine strength. When it comes to effective inspirational speaking, it's not just *what* you know, it's *Who* you know! Words linked with the Spirit's power are a spiritual dynamic. Notice the combination: "my message" and "my preaching."

High Calling

Spirit inspiration is the "batteries included." Without inspiration, words and phrases are mere letters and punctuation marks stacked in a neat pile. Inspiration gives impressionable form. The apostle John wrote about the inspiration of the moment in his second letter: "I have much to write to you, but I do not want to use paper and ink. Instead, I hope to visit you and talk with you face to face, so that our joy may be complete" (2 John 12).

Of course, the apostle was a gifted writer—gifted by the Holy Spirit—but he also recognized the importance of public speaking. He had "much to write." His heart was filled with his message. But he had to make a choice in delivering the message: "I do not want to use paper and ink."

You will make many choices as a public speaker. But perhaps your greatest speaking choices will be those of improving your speaking skills and your message content. It's a high calling. Media consultant Timothy J. Koegel wrote, "I find it fascinating that when conducting presentation skills and training sessions, the better the presenter, the more they soak up the material. Perhaps it's because these individuals understand that: How the word is spoken can dramatically impact the power of the spoken word."[2]

Of course, this book isn't the last word—or the final word. My brother Terry says I've never had a thought I didn't put in print. But hopefully this will be an introduction to the exciting world of inspirational speaking.

—Stan Toler, 2009

The Speaker's Presentation

Every presentation is a once-in-a-lifetime opportunity.

1

RESEARCH YOUR PRESENTATION

Homework is at least 80 percent of the speaking assignment.

A little boy in Sunday School was concentrating on his drawing during the activity time when the teacher suddenly stood over his shoulder. There on the big sheet of paper was a picture of two stick figures. One figure, with outstretched hands, was standing by a brown-colored truck with large letters on the side: "U-P-S." Another figure was in the driver's seat, handing a package out the window.

"Timmy, that's an interesting picture," the teacher said, "but what does that have to do with today's lesson?" Without looking up, Timmy continued to draw and answered, "It's God delivering the Ten Commandments to Moses."[1]

Speaking isn't just about the delivery. Obviously little Timmy hadn't done his homework. Homework is at least 80 percent of the speaking assignment. Unlike that term paper in high school, doing research for your speaking assignment involves more than collecting the thoughts of others and recording them on 3-by-5 note cards. (Where were the environmentalists when you needed them? Just think of all the trees that gave their life so those students could impress their teachers with note cards! Now they collect URL addresses!)

Researching your speaking assignment is a bit more holistic. It includes factors other than collecting the wit and wisdom of living or dead celebrities and putting them on paper or in a file folder. It includes

1. Motive

Why are you making your presentation?

If you are a vocational minister, you're probably fulfilling your pastoral agreement: no speak, no check. Every other speaker may fall into the volunteered, recruited, or appointed categories. Whatever the assignment, as a Christian speaker, you are a spokesperson for the Kingdom. You are the messenger of God's truth. Your speaking is having an eternal influence.

Your motives must come from the truth you present. Jesus said, "For out of the overflow of the heart the mouth speaks" (Matt. 12:34). Check your motive:

- Am I seeking to promote self or am I seeking to exalt Jesus Christ?
- Am I seeking to impress others more than I am seeking to impress Jesus Christ?
- Can I speak with a heart of love for the audience?
- How will I show God's eternal purpose in my speaking?
- Will I depend on my own skills rather than on the Holy Spirit's anointing?

Dale Carnegie said, "Be more concerned with your character than with your reputation."[2]

2. Topic

Whether you are preaching a Christmas message to a packed church auditorium or speaking to a small group in your community, your topic is important. Among other things, it may have been the thing that drew your audience in the first place.

There is a classic story about the preacher who announced he was preaching on the Top 20 Sins. One good ol' boy from the community said to his buddy, "I think I'm going to that service just to make sure I haven't missed any of 'em!" If that preacher had simply announced he was speaking about sin, the adventurer might not have been as interested. He would have just assumed—and rightly so—that the preacher was against it.

Here are some things about the topic that you can't miss when you speak in public:

- **Make sure it is focused.** Most audiences can handle only one subject at a time. Try to avoid side trips and detours.

Building your presentation from intro to main points to transitions to conclusion should keep you on the speaking straight and narrow.

- **Make sure it fits.** Trying on a topic before you wear it in public will make for a more comfortable experience for the audience, and for you. For example, if your audience knows that you are not mechanically minded, choosing the topic "How to Change Your Transmission Without Breaking a Sweat" probably won't wear that well. Ed Foreman said, "Talk about what you know about and you'll never have anything to worry about."

- **Make sure it is relevant.** Touch the audience where it lives. A 20-minute speech on the virtues of eight-track recording tapes probably won't draw a huge crowd. Make sure your topic links to the knowledge, experience, and need of the audience.

- **Make sure it has a good title.** "Topic" and "title" lean on each other for support. Of the books that I have written, one stands out as a favorite. It isn't a favorite just because of the content—or because it has been a best-selling book. It is a favorite because of the title: *God Has Never Failed Me, but He's Sure Scared Me to Death a Few Times.* The title should be eye-catching and thought-provoking.

3. Material

I heard of a preacher who could thrill an audience simply by saying the word "Mesopotamia." Now there had to be some public speaking skills there, but if you weren't a big fan of the word "Mesopotamia," you probably wouldn't get a lot out of the message. Choosing the right material is a key to reaching your audience.

Starting with a Bible text or passage automatically puts you on good ground. But even there, you'll want to make sure your audience is familiar with the text or passage. Biblical illiteracy is a sweeping problem in our church culture.

It's wise not to assume that everyone knows the story of Daniel in the lions' den. Often it takes only the introduction to a familiar Bible narrative, and the blank stares of the audience, to know everyone's not sailing on the same sea. When preparing your material, you'll want to keep some important things in mind:

- **It must be biblically and theologically sound.** For example, if you're doing a series of messages on the Book of Revelation, you'll want to make sure you read (and quote from) commentaries by theologians who are recognized by your denomination.

- **It must be familiar to the audience.** You will have only a few seconds to make a connection with your audience. If you start with the unfamiliar—and stay there, you'll be speaking to yourself, and perhaps your spouse.

- **It must be varied in content.** Your job as a public speaker is to present a buffet, not just an appetizer. When you prepare your material, you will want to think of a variety of ways you can communicate truths, including illustrations and objects—"doors and windows," ways that it can be applied.

- **It must have a good beginning and a good ending.** Planning your introduction and conclusion up front will save you a lot of time in making the connection and the application. I once heard a speaker say that the first and last 30 seconds are crucial to your presentation.

- **It must have a logical path.** Your audience likely won't be holding a GPS in their hands. You'll need to show them how to transition from Point A to Point B. And you will need to give them a place to rest along the way. The last thing you want said of your presentation is "Huh?"

4. Environment

You'll also need to do your homework on the speaking environment. If at all possible, do a walk-through of the location in which you are speaking. Make some mental notes—if not written:

- **How is the lighting?** Is the stage or presentation area well lit? If not, you will have to do some walking around to make a visible connection to the audience. Where are the light switches? You may need to ask someone to "get the lights" during your PowerPoint presentation. Like you, he or she may be new to the area.

- **What is the seating configuration?** Is it circular, semicircular, or front-to-back? The configuration will determine what techniques you will use in making eye contact with the audience, or in projecting your message to the back row.

- **How is the room temperature?** Of course, the temperature will change according to the wishes of the building engineer—or the whims of that "one in every crowd"—but getting a feel for the temperature of the room, and the obvious ventilation, will give you a better idea of the extremes you may have to deal with.

- **Where are the "facilities"?** Just in case you need to make a quick trip in between the announcements, the offering, or the roll call, it would be wise to know you won't have to walk a half mile to the restroom.

- **Who is in charge?** Meeting and greeting your host or hostess in advance of your presentation is a plus. That meeting will tell you a lot about the event audience—and give you an opportunity to ask questions about media, lighting, and time constraints.

5. Media

Planning for multimedia presentations *in advance* will be as helpful to you as it will to the staff that will be assisting you.

- **Know your media.** Find out if you need to bring a data projector, for instance. Is there a pull-down screen, a rear-view projection screen, or a plain wall that could be used as a screen?

- **Know your technician.** In case you are fortunate to have an assistant, try to connect with that person before the event. Tell him or her the kind of media you will be using and then ask about his or her experience with that media.

- **Know your material.** Make sure your presentation is in logical and sequential order.

- **Know your options.** Remember, you're in "sales" not "management." You can't control the weather; you can only talk about it. A sudden thunderstorm may change your presentation. What is your plan B? Is there emergency lighting? Are there other media—such as a flip chart or white board—available in case of equipment malfunction?

- **Know your limits.** Don't "over-media." The Master didn't have video clips, but He got His point across, even when He was standing in a boat on the Sea of Galilee. Use media familiar to you when you communicate your message.

📁 *File Folder*

PowerPoint Tips

If you will be making a PowerPoint presentation, save the graphics for last. Write an outline first. Then roughly storyboard the presentation on several blank pieces of paper. Believe me, this is a huge time saver. Talk the storyboard out loud and make sure it flows and makes sense before preparing the PowerPoint slides. Do not get carried away with PowerPoint graphics, colors, or animation. Use them only if they enhance your message.

—Elise Bauer[3]

📁 *File Folder*

Handouts

Have handouts ready and give them out at the appropriate time. Tell audience ahead of time that you will be giving out an outline of your presentation so that they will not waste time taking unnecessary notes during your presentation.[4]

6. Technique

Whether you're choosing bagels or making a speech, variety is a good thing. A dull speaker can turn an exciting subject into a marathon. Learn methods for keeping audience attention.

"Go to school" on some of your favorite speakers. What techniques do they use? How do they deliver their main thoughts? What introductions and conclusions do they use? If it works, work it!

There are some generic techniques that will help you make a positive impression on your audience—and help you get your message across:

- **Use gestures.** Sometimes the best way to get your point across is to point. In his prime, there wasn't a public speaker any better at using gestures than Dr. Billy Graham. His hands and arms were constantly in motion. They emphasized a point, expressed a geographical area, drew attention to the Bible, and reached out to the audience. Gestures help your audience focus on your presentation. Statues don't communicate; people communicate. I remember watching traffic police in South Africa. I was amazed at how they communicated without saying a word. Just the motion of their arms gave direction.

- **Move around.** Body movement has the same effect as hand gestures. It can be used to emphasize a point, refocus the audience, and create a sense of intimacy. For example, moving toward the audience suggests a more personal communication. In fact, moving from the stage to the front row of the audience often helps to break down the "geographical wall" between the speaker and the listener.

- **Use media.** Often an application of truth can be conveyed secondhand. You've seen how ventriloquists can say things through a dummy that they could never say themselves. The puppet is communicating the message. PowerPoint slides or video or audio clips can be used to reinforce a point or make an application. Jesus was adept at using inanimate objects to teach eternal truths. Vineyards, lilies, mustard seeds, mountains, and trees were the media of His day—and worked effectively to teach spiritual truths.

- **Use the pause.** A "pregnant pause" can give birth to effective communication. Without "laboring" the subject, let me say that a pause during your presentation is a dynamic technique. First, it will give importance to what has just been said. Second, it will give the audience a chance to breathe and reflect. Third, it will give a sense of credibility and authority to the speaker.

- **Vary the tone of voice.** Actors communicate not only with body movement but also with the pitch and volume of their voice. Vary the tone of voice according to the message. Use louder volumes to emphasize a point. Use softer volumes to draw listener attention. Change the tone of your voice to avoid a "monotone" delivery.

- **Use quotes and illustrations.** I learned storytelling from the best. It was an art form where I grew up. Mountaineers in West Virginia didn't have cable TV; they *were* cable TV! The drama, suspense, and humor in the stories I heard as a child made me fall in love with the art of using quotes and illustrations as bridges to reach people.

Every presentation is a once-in-a-lifetime opportunity. There will never be another moment like the one you will have when you speak. The audience will never be the same, the atmosphere will be totally different, and the weather will have changed. You have this moment. You are the steward of this time. So use it wisely and be prepared.

 ## *File Folder*

Meaningful Pauses

Leaving a moment of silence between sentences can be a powerful public speaking tool. Pausing after an important point or before answering a question will help to hold the audience's attention. A pause can also give you time to formulate your next statement.[5]

File Folder

Gestures

Good gestures help underline what is said.
- Elbow movement gives strength to gestures.
- Wrist movement conveys precision.
- Hands contain power and control.[6]

File Folder

Choosing Quotations

Support your message with quotations and testimonials. Here are some tips:
- Make sure the person quoted has high visibility and credibility.
- Choose a quotation from someone who is politically "safe."
- Avoid trite or overused quotations.
- Keep the quotation in context—don't add or delete for convenience' sake.
- Choose quotations that are both factual and emotional.
- Choose quotations based on their strength, relevance, and impact.

2
ENGAGE YOUR AUDIENCE

Pay attention to your audience and it will pay attention to you.

Acclaimed speaker and presenter Mark Sanborn said, "There is no excuse for 'winging it.' The best speakers are borderline neurotic in their preparation—even if their demeanor suggests otherwise. Presenters who come across as brilliantly unscripted likely spent hours practicing in order to appear 'off the cuff.'"[1]

Next to your delivery, research is the key to a better speech. If you've seen me speak in person, you've probably seen one of my top 10 lists on an overhead screen. Of course I'm not the first to use them, but I find them to be an effective way to make an instant connection with the audience. And connection is what public speaking is all about. You are going into the assignment with a plan—perhaps answering the question, "So what?"

S—Start with a theme.
O—Organize your speech.
W—Watch your words.
H—Have fun with the audience.
A—Allow enough time.
T—Tell it with enthusiasm.

But all the preparation is useless without an audience. You don't want to end up talking to yourself! Just as "the customer is first" in retail, in public speaking "the audience is first."

Pay attention to your audience and they will pay attention to you. Give the audience a top priority in your preparation and delivery. When possible, get to know the members of your audience, speak to them, and connect with them. I always do a lot of *hand-*

shakes and "howdies" with audience members before a speaking presentation. I find that when I have made a connection in advance of the presentation, I am already a step ahead.

Your future, whether a couple of minutes or a lifetime, will depend on your relationship to your listeners. And as you know, relationships take work. Zig Ziglar said, "You don't pay the price for success; you enjoy the price of success . . . you pay the price for failure."[2] Your extra effort in knowing your listeners will go a long way in making the connection with them.

- What brings us together?
- What do we have in common?
- How can I touch them through my message?

Getting to know your listeners is a science that differs with each situation. Your 20-minute speech to a service club, nonprofit, or corporate event probably won't allow you a great deal of time to research the audience. On the other hand, your tenure as a pastor or teacher in your local church setting will give you added time in learning the ins and outs of the audience.

Audience evaluation, either short or longer term, will have several of the same guidelines:

 **File Folder**

Speaking Basics

There are basic things that you can do to ensure that your verbal messages are understood—and remembered—time and time again.

- Understand the purpose of the presentation.
- Keep the message clear and concise.
- Be prepared.
- Be vivid when delivering the message.[3]

1. Know the Boundaries. Speakers have a lot in common with volleyball players: if they don't stay in bounds, they'll lose their chance to serve.

Time boundaries. If you've been given 25 minutes on the program, your 45-minute presentation will probably be your last presentation to that organization! We live in a time-restraint culture. Haddon W. Robinson said, "Preachers address an audience that comes to church with clickers in their head. . . . they vote in the first thirty seconds whether to tune in or turn off the channel."[4]

As a general rule, you can put 150 words into a minute of speaking.

Subject boundaries. If you want to stay in hot water, float your speaking boat on the tides of politics, stereotypes, cultural put-downs, and authority-bashing.

Room boundaries. When folks start fanning themselves with your handouts, you know it's time to either open a window, or as Moses said, "Let my people go." Keep your eyes on the room temperature-audience reaction ratio.

2. Know the Demographics. What kinds of people will be in the majority during your speaking presentation? If you have access to those listener demographics, and they are usually available from the event host, you will have a head start on speaking success.

- **What will be the audience size?** Smaller audiences call for a more personalized presentation—including time for questions and answers, and comments. Larger to megalarge audiences call for a more general and more physically dynamic presentation—including larger gestures, more body movement, and larger support media.

- **What is their gender?** How you will personally relate to your audience members will depend on whether or not you are one of them—and when it comes to gender, there's a 50-50 chance you are! The stories and quotations you use are often gender-related. For example, a men's group may not relate to the history of embroidery. But watch their eyes light up when you use a story about the quarterback on their favorite football team!

- **What is the average age?** If you've ever tried to teach the genealogy of the Old Testament kings to a junior high class, you've probably learned the importance of age-specific material. About the time you think the class knows who King Hezekiah is, they will have created enough paper airplanes from lesson sheets to give military air support to a third-world country. Learn what reaches persons of each age level. Hint: talk to children, youth, or adult ministers. Their insights will keep you from stubbing your toe on a speech cement parking barrier.

3. Speak to Needs. Depending on your audience demographics, the scope of needs will be wide. Christian leader and preacher James O. Davis said, "Many ministers of the Gospel spend most of their time thinking about what they are going to say to the audience, yet the average person is persuaded more by feelings than by facts. Mannerisms, gestures, head movements, facial expressions, platform movement, eye contact and clothing project the overall presence of the presenter."[5]

- **Obvious needs.** Remember, you have the answer your audience is looking for—otherwise, your listeners would have opted for a trip to the coffee shop. And you only have to take an occasional glance at a newspaper, newsmagazine, or cable news show to know what they are thinking about. Don't play hide and seek with the elephant in the room. If contemporary affairs isn't the main subject, at least put it in the introduction or conclusion.

- **Hidden needs.** You are an important speaker because you are human. You know what humans encounter on a daily basis. As you speak with positive words and energetic energy, you are giving your audience a human, psychological safety net. You are convincing them of their importance, of their personal worth, of their contribution to society. Always leave people in a better state than you found them!

📁 *File Folder*

Dynamic

Perhaps the best way to convey dynamism is to have a genuine interest in both your topic and your audience. When you are authentic and real, your dynamism is naturally present. Allow your nervousness to catapult you to a heightened sense of awareness of your surroundings and your audience.

- Embrace your nervousness.
- Practice gestures and movements.
- Use visual aids to add interest to your talk.
- Let go of your self-consciousness and focus on your audience and your message.

🗁 *File Folder*

Speed and Volume of Delivery

- Vary the speed of your delivery
- Fast to excite and stimulate
- Slow to emphasize and control
- Use increased volume to get attention
- Speaking quietly conveys confidentiality and sincerity to what you're saying[6]

3
ACHIEVE YOUR SPEAKING OBJECTIVES

*Your audience must feel comfortable enough with you
to hear even the toughest truths from you.*

Business consultant and speaker Michael Heath encourages public speakers to PANIC!

There is nothing like a bit of PANIC to get you started on the road to making successful and effective presentations!

P = Purpose

You must make sure you have both a purpose and a clear objective for your presentation.

A = Audience

Make sure you know everything there is to know about your audience.

N = Need

What information will the audience need? What will you need in the way of information to make this presentation successful?

I = Information

Make 2 key points in a 20 minutes slot, 3 key points in a 30 minutes slot and 4 key points in a 40 minutes slot.

C = Communication

We all absorb information through one of three ways:
Visually—through our sight
Aurally—through our ears
Kinesthetically—through our physical involvement.[1]

As you can see from the PANIC advice, there are some goals and objectives that all speakers should consider—not just for them, but for their audiences. Part of your speaking assignment is to help your audience reach its goals: spiritual, intellectual, emotional, relational, or financial.

Actress Lily Tomlin had a comedy routine that portrayed her as Ernestine the telephone operator. One of her lines became very popular: "Is this the party to whom I'm speaking?" How would you answer? "Shotgun speaking" may fulfill the contract, but it doesn't fulfill the goal.

What is the main point of your presentation? What is the audience takeaway? How will you engage/connect with your audience? You must make a connection in the following areas:

1. Spiritual. People are born not only with a tendency to disobey God but also with an urgency to love Him—and to be loved by Him. What truth will you present that will cause your audience members to reflect on their relationship with God?

2. Intellectual. Your presentation will give your audience an opportunity to grow in knowledge. What principle do you want them to take away? What facts will you give to provoke their learning processes?

3. Emotional. Your audience must feel comfortable enough *with you* to hear even the toughest truths *from* you. How will you let them know you really like them?

4. Relational. A common audience goal is to be affirmed or accepted. Any "holier than thou" attitude should be abandoned. Note that you will convey attitude by your expression, posture, and tone of voice. Bridge the relational gap with a story. Affirm. Love. Connect.

5. Financial. Your presentation can actually inspire someone to a better standard of living! Your motivation, insights, and practical experience can be just the thing to move someone off financial center.

The task of public speaking is often daunting. Along the way to a strong finish, you'll have to work your way around the cone zones of human laziness, spiritual doubt, equipment failure, interruptions, roller-coaster room temperatures, and stereotypes. But finish strong.

After you've told them what you will be telling them; tell them; and then tell them what you told them. Timothy J. Koegel says, "What you say last will be remembered more. . . . a purpose statement is an effective way to end your presentation. The purpose statement provides the one, two or three key points your audience must remember as they leave the room. The shorter and more direct the purpose statement, the greater the impact."[2]

🗁 *File Folder*

Analyzing Your Presentation

The beginning of excellence is the elimination of foolishness. You can ramp up your speaking performance by analyzing your last presentation with these seven questions:

1. Did I stick to my allotted time?
2. Did I develop and present purposefully?
3. Was I thoroughly prepared?
4. Did I capture attention at the very beginning?
5. Did I positively influence listeners?
6. Was I appropriately entertaining, or at least not boring?
7. Did I end only once?[3]

4

CONNECT WITH THE SENSES

A pile of facts has no warmth unless it is set on fire.

No, the "five senses" isn't the amount left in your checking account after you've paid your bills! God built sensors into His creation that react to various stimuli. A wise speaker will use those sensors. And a good presentation will appeal to the five sensors/senses. How will you convey the sense of seeing, touching, smelling, tasting, and hearing? You will have an opportunity to paint or sculpt or cook with your words. Use your artistic skill.

In their book *Preaching That Connects* Mark Galli and Craig Brian Larson give us some questions we can ask about our message. Among them are:

- How should this text affect the way my listeners live tomorrow?
- What are the word pictures in this text, and how can I use them as a running scenery in the sermon?
- What felt needs and real needs does this text address?
- How have I experienced the truth of this text?
- How do I define the key words or ideas?
- What emotions are touched by this text?
- Have there been any stories in the news lately that relate to this subject?[1]

There are at least three ways you can connect with senses:

1. Verbally. Storytelling is a craft that will be your speaking bread and butter. Isn't it amazing how this techno-savvy culture, with enough electronic gadgets to send someone to the moon and back—and play country music in their earphones during the trip—is still captivated by a well-told story? Who knows, it might go all the way back to those nursery rhymes told to us before the house lights were dimmed and the night-lights came on? Many of us, just before we were advised not to "let the bedbugs bite," were transported to the fairer and brighter and softer world of a bedtime story.

No one ever told a story the way Jesus did. He used the common and ordinary experiences of life to convey the heavenly graces. On one occasion, five thousand people were so thrilled to be able to hear His storytelling that they even forgot to pack a lunch. Notice how His stories appealed to the senses, with their emphasis on the sights and smells and tastes and touches of the land of the Bible.

In my book *Stan Toler's Practical Guide for Pastoral Ministry*, I give some guidelines for storytelling. The story must be

- Biblical. It has a definite tie to a scriptural truth.
- Believable. It must relate to the experience of your audience.
- Logical. The path from the introduction to the conclusion is plainly marked.
- Practical. It has an obvious reason for being there.
- Emotional. It appeals to the senses.
- Valuable. It has an "aha" factor.
- Transferable. It has meaning.[2]

2. Visually. You may think that props are an invention of postmodern worshippers. Not so. Even before the first classic car was pushed onto a stage as a visual for a contemporary preacher's message, props were an established method of communicating truth and connecting with the senses (remember the Ebenezer Stone, 1 Sam. 7:12?).

📁 *File Folder*

Props

Props help warm up the audience when you do a public speaking engagement. They can be used as a substitute for notes. They help focus attention on the speaking points you are trying to make along with illustrating them for you. They make better connections than your words with the visually oriented members of your audience. They create interest, add variety, and make your points more memorable.[3]

3. Spiritually. President Theodore Roosevelt was asked what he felt was the "single factor that accounted for his popularity with the public. Roosevelt replied, 'To put into words what is in their hearts and minds, but not in their mouth.'"[4]

It's the "I get it!" moment. It's the point when audience members nod in approval. You have touched not only their heads with knowledge but also their hearts with inspiration. Spirit connects with spirit. It's a worthy goal of every speaker. A pile of facts has no warmth unless it is set on fire.

Make sure you make the application. Give the audience a "bridge" to your idea—something they can experience personally. Whether you use a story, quotation, or a joke, make sure it "seals the deal." Show the audience, "This is how this idea works in real life."

Make sure the application supports the message. Again, what is your main point, the value-added principle? What one thing do you want your audience to take away from your presentation? That's where the link is made. We have too many ideas and ideals to sort through on a given day. If it's not a TV talk on the benefits of a toaster oven, it will probably be the necessity of a brand-name cough suppressant. Give the audience a break; serve one course at a time—and don't forget dessert.

Make sure the application has doors and windows. You are the artist; the audience is your patron. They need to "experience" your presentation. It must sing to them, talk to them, and woo them with its beauty. Ed Stetzer said of preaching, "At the heart of effective preaching is a solid missiological perspective. Are you communicating in such a way that your words actually convey biblical truth to your audience? Or does your preaching float right past your hearers because it's not delivered 'on a frequency' that they listen to?"[5]

🗁 *File Folder*

Illustration

An illustration can be a story, a likeness or even a physical object. The important element of an illustration is that it creates some kind of response whether it be emotional or intellectually in your audience. And the goal of your illustration is to move away from just speaking words to creating mental images in the minds of your listeners that can be associated with your topic.[6]

🗁 *File Folder*

Quick Tips

- Don't drink too much caffeine before giving your speech—it tends to give people the shakes, and nerves will make this worse.
- Preparation prevents panic—knowing your material well will really boost your confidence.
- If you make a mistake, don't worry. The chances are the audience didn't notice. If it is obvious, don't apologize, simply make the correction and continue with the rest of your speech.
- Remember—no matter how large an audience seems—it is made up of individuals.[7]

🗁 *File Folder*

Pop Culture Illustrations

To use pop culture illustrations well I must do two things. I must answer the two questions that the pop culture person has. Number one, do you know about my world? Number two, do you care about my world? If I want to use pop culture illustrations well and gain credibility, I have to demonstrate that I know something about that world and that I care about the people in that world.[8]

—Kevin A. Miller

5

HELP YOUR AUDIENCE REACH ITS GOALS

No matter how many jokes you throw in, public speaking is serious business.

Henry O. Dormann said, "Artistry with words is more of a skill than artistry with paints. A painter can correct and redefine and add subtle tones to what he uses his brush to do, but spoken words are final. As they leave the tongue, they are finished and cast forever, no matter what other words may follow."[1]

Every morning I pray the same prayer from the Psalms: "Let the words of my mouth, and the meditation of my heart, be acceptable in thy sight, O LORD, my strength, and my redeemer" (Ps. 19:14, KJV). On some days I will be doing a TV interview in the morning and two or three radio interviews in the afternoon. Then, before catching the sports on the late news, I'll be speaking to an audience at a seminar or a conference. A long time ago I realized the responsibility of public speaking. Long-term attitudes and eternal decisions are on the line.

I wish I could let you off the hook, but I can't. No matter how many jokes you throw in, public speaking is serious business. That's why you shouldn't approach it without some goals in mind:

- Preparation goals—30 to 60 minutes of research for every presentation minute.

- Time goals—3- to 5-minute introduction, 25- to 30-minute main points, and 3- to 5-minute conclusion and application.
- Spiritual goals—pray for God's wisdom, leadership, and giftedness.
- Ministry goals—immediate and long-term follow-up with interested audience members.

There are goals for the audience as well. Audience members may not be writing on score cards—if you're lucky—but even before you tap the microphone to see if it's "on," they will have decided what they will expect from you. Your audience will have at least four goals that they presume you will help them reach:

1. Understanding. Your audience expects you to understand them. They expect you to get under their skin, to feel their pain or experience their joy.

2. Improvement. I don't know what they will pay to hear you speak (personally, I've been known to exercise my right of free speech!), but I do know that they expect to be better off for listening to you. Your practical and biblical instruction will enlighten them.

3. Recognition. Your audience expects a little R-E-S-P-E-C-T, as Aretha Franklin might say. Many have been browbeaten before they arrived in the auditorium. Some have little or no confidence in their right to be a citizen of planet Earth. Their goal is to be recognized as a dues-paid member of God's created kingdom.

4. Safety. They've already been threatened by the system—systematically. They want you to make them feel safe. They want to know that it is OK to live against the grain of society. They want to know that beliefs are worth living and dying for. The opportunity of a lifetime is yours—each time you speak.

Joseph Addison said it well, "If the minds of men were laid open we should see but little difference between that of the wise man and that of a fool. The difference is that the first knows how to pick and cull his thoughts for conversation . . . whereas the other lets them all indifferently fly out in words."[2] It's true, when it comes to the bottom line, what you say comes from who you are. Jesus' words still ring the bell, "Out of the heart, man speaks" (see Luke 6:45).

☐ *File Folder*
Causes of Public Speaking Stress

- Thinking that public speaking is inherently stressful (it's not).
- Thinking you need to be brilliant or perfect to succeed (you don't).
- Trying to impart too much information or cover too many points in a short presentation.
- Having the wrong purpose in mind (to get rather than to give/contribute).
- Trying to please everyone (this is unrealistic).
- Trying to emulate other speakers (very difficult) rather than simply being yourself (very easy).[3]

—Morton C. Orman, M.D.

☐ *File Folder*
Using Notes

Use note cards. Include quotes, statistics, and lists you may need, *not* paragraphs of text.

- Number your note cards! (Just in case you drop them).
- Don't put too much information on each note card or you will find yourself reading too much. Put only a few words or key phrases.
- Leave your notes on the lectern or table and move away occasionally. Don't be afraid to move away from your notes and get out of your comfort zone.
- Use pictures or picture maps to guide yourself. Pictures help you to "visualize" the key points of your speech. Use mental pictures as well to tell the story in your head. This will take some creativity, but will be worth the effort.[4]

—Lenny Laskowski

SECTION TWO

The Speaker's Tools

Always leave people in a better state than when you found them!

6
ONLINE RESOURCES

(Note: The author doesn't necessarily endorse the beliefs or products of all Web sites, articles, or organizations listed.)

Public Speaking

Act Now
http://www.actnow.com.au/Tool/Tips_on_public_speaking.aspx

Allyn & Bacon Public Speaking Web Site
http://wps.ablongman.com/ab_public_speaking_2/

Elise Bauer
http://www.elise.com/web/a/public_speaking_tips.php

Famous Speeches
http://www.famousquotes.me.uk/speeches/index.htm

How Stuff Works
http://www.howstuffworks.com/18-tips-for-public-speaking.htm

Lenny Laskowski
http://www.ljlseminars.com/monthtip.htm

Management Help
http://www.managementhelp.org/commskls/presntng/presntng.htm

Mind Tools
http://www.mindtools.com/CommSkll/PublicSpeaking.htm

Presentation Helper
http://www.presentationhelper.co.uk

Professional Business Communications
http://www.professional-business-communications.com/articles/pubs/

Projectors Solution
http://www.projectorsolution.com/effectivepresentations.asp?

PowerPoint Presentations
http://www.presentationhelper.co.uk/microsoft-powerpoint.htm

Public Speaking Institute
http://www.public-speaking.org

Public Speaking Tip
   http://www.publicspeakingtip.org/
Ron St. John
   http://www.hawaii.edu/mauispeech/html/speech_151.html
Strategicomm
   http://www.strategiccomm.com/usecharts.html
Toastmasters
   http://www.toastmasters.org
United Nations Association
   http://www.unausa.org/site/pp.asp?c=fvKRI8MPJpF&b=457149

Preaching
Christianity Today
   http://www.christianitytoday.com/bible/features/sermonhelps.html
Desperate Preacher
   http://www.desperatepreacher.com
Nazarene Publishing House
   www.nph.com
Preaching
   http://www.preaching.com/resources/preacher_to_preacher
   /11546984/
Preaching Today
   http://www.preachingtoday.com
REV!
   http://rev.org
Sermon Central
   http://www.sermoncentral.com
Sermon Index
   http://www.sermonindex.net
Wesleyan Publishing House
   www.wesleyan.org/wph
Your Church
   http://www.christianitytoday.com/cbg

Author Site
Stan Toler
   www.stantoler.com

7

ANALYSIS

📁 *File Folder*

What Do I Want to Accomplish?

To speak to the whole person, I must ask account for the hearer's intellect, emotions, and will. I want to do more than inform the intellect. I want to touch emotion and challenge the will. What do I want my audience to think? What do I want them to feel? What do I want them to do?

—Gregory Hollifield[1]

Analyzing Your Presentation

1. Approximately how much time did I spend on preparation?

2. Did the audience connect with my stories? Why or why not?

3. Did the audience respond to my humor? Why or why not?

4. Did I focus on the main point(s)?

5. Did I support my main point(s) with subpoints?

6. What gestures did I use during the majority of the presentation?

7. Did I stay within the allotted time?

8. What visuals did I use?

9. Did I make eye contact with persons in each area of the room?

10. What connection did I make with the audience during my introduction?

11. How did I make the application of my main point(s)?

12. Was my dress appropriate for the occasion?

13. How did my body movement reflect my interest or energy?

14. Did I vary the tone and volume of my voice?

15. Approximately how much time did I spend in spiritual preparation?

8

SPEAKER HELPS

On Occasion

Advent

Humor

"Cash or Credit?"

My brother Terry often tells about a small girl who had shopped all day with her grandma. Grandma, seeking good behavior, promised a trip to see Santa at the end of the day. The little girl was good, and the reward was given. Santa gave the little girl a candy cane.

"What do you say to Santa?" Grandma asked.

At first the little girl looked perplexed. Then with a knowing smile she said, "Charge it." —Stan Toler

Churches and Christmas

Two friends were riding on a city bus. One of the riders saw a billboard sign sponsored by a local church: KEEP CHRIST IN CHRISTMAS.

"Well, have you ever . . . ?" the rider said to her friend, "Now the churches are sticking their noses into Christmas!"

—Source unknown

Holiday Plans

One family was discussing their holiday plans. Father gave his plan: "Let's hang some things up."

"What things?" his teenage daughter asked.

He answered, "Mistletoe, stockings, and your cell phone!"

—Source unknown

Post Office Prepares for Christmas

"Here's some good news out of Washington, D.C. The post office says it is ready for the big holiday Christmas crush of mail. They have already placed an order for 10 million new signs that will read: 'This Window Closed.'"

—*The Late Show with David Letterman*

Stars or Rats?

Judy had one small but important part in the children's Christmas party. She was to hold up the word "Star" at the appropriate time.

It seemed pretty simple—childproof, if you will. The letters were cut out and attached to a stick. Judy's assignment was to raise the stick with letters S-T-A-R on it. When the time came, the little girl, right on cue, held the stick high. The audience roared with laughter.

At first the proud mother thought the congregation was appreciating her cute daughter. Then she realized why they were really laughing. You see, no one had told the little girl that there was a right way and a wrong way to hold the stick. Consequently, when she raised the stick, the sign was backward. Instead of saying S-T-A-R, the sign said R-A-T-S.

—Stan Toler

Illustrations

Family Advent Worship

The Advent season is a time of celebration and hope. Gather your family and place an Advent wreath on the table. Within the evergreen circle place three purple candles, one rose-colored candle, and a large white candle. The following worship schedule can then be observed:

WEEK ONE: Read Matt. 3:1-2; light a purple (prophecy) candle and have family prayer. Discussion: Expectations and hopes for the future.

WEEK TWO: Read Matt. 2:1-6; light a purple (shepherd) candle and have family prayer. Discussion: Anticipation and preparation for Christmas.

WEEK THREE: Read Luke 2:8-12; light a rose-colored (angel) candle and have family prayer. Discussion: Our joys in life.

WEEK FOUR: Read Matt. 2:7-11; light a purple (magi) candle and have family prayer. Discussion: Good gifts from the Father.

CHRISTMAS DAY: Light the Christ candle and give thanks for Jesus, the Light of the World.   —Linda Toler

Step Out of the Frame

A young boy, the son of missionaries, was living in a boarding school. Unable to visit his parents for the Christmas holidays, one of the dorm parents asked the boy what he wanted for Christmas.

He picked up a picture of his father from a stand by his bed, pointed to it, and said, "I want him to step out of that frame and stand by me."[1]   —E. Stanley Jones

The Advent Adventure

The words "Advent" and "adventure" have a common derivation. Advent should be a season of Christian adventure. As Christmas approaches, new hope and new faith enter our hearts. The adventure of life is renewed and reinvigorated. A spirit of expectancy and enthusiasm comes to those who remember the hope that God in Christ brings to man.[2]

The Gift of Forgiveness

After describing a nostalgic Christmas Eve, with the family gathered together around the Christmas tree, singing carols, and eating Christmas goodies before attending the Candlelight Service, the author reminds us that for some families, Christmas Eve turns out to be a great battlefield. There is no peace on earth, much less in the home. Expectations often run high and disappointments deep. The gift hoped for is the gift never given. The son who said he would be there—isn't. The sister who never has a kind word for anyone starts one of her many tirades.

Then he advises, "Wrap up one more gift and give it away—the gift of forgiveness. It may be the most important, and most beautiful, gift you will ever give to another person."[3]

Wise Worship

My old friend Harry Childers once remarked, "After the wise men had truly worshipped, they opened their treasures." Hearing that,

I made an important discovery on my journey to Christmas. You see, I had always wondered what happened to the gifts the wise men brought to the Son of God. Through Harry's observation I was reminded that God's guidance is perfect.

God sent Mary, Joseph, and the Christ child to Bethlehem. When they arrived, they were in great need of food, finances, and shelter. They had moved from the lowly stable to a temporary home. It appeared that Satan's diabolical scheme for Herod to murder babies was going to succeed. But according to my friend Harry, after the wise men worshiped the Savior, they opened their treasures and unwittingly financed the flight of the Son of God to Egypt. Thus, they thwarted Herod's efforts to kill Mary and Joseph's firstborn son.

Here's my discovery: wise worship always leads to miracles, spiritual breakthroughs, and provisions from the hand of almighty God! And, wise worship only occurs when we, like the wise men, are willing to release our gifts to the Lord. Once that release has happened, we never know how the Father will use those gifts.

—Stan Toler

Witnesses to the Light

A celebrity speaker and well-known musician joined a prison ministry team for revival services in the prison. The team also included an ex-convict who gave a personal testimony of his faith in the Lord Jesus Christ.

At the close of the services, several inmates reflected on the revival. A Muslim inmate shared his appreciation for the celebrity team members who took the time to come to the prison. But he added, "Frankly, I was more impressed with the brother on the team who sat at our table after the service and ate a meal with us. That's what really got to me."

More witnesses to the light wear aprons than minks.[4]

Quotes

A True Celebration of Advent

No matter how commercial Advent and Christmas become, we are still in control of our own lives. It can be made sacred and spiritual if we make the preparations for Christmas a true celebration of Advent—a time of reflection on the beautiful mystery of the birth of Christ.[5]

Advent Invocation

As we enter this Advent season,

May we find it to be beautiful, a time of glowing lights and bright colors.

May we find it to be happy, a time of smiles and bright faces.

May we find it to be heartwarming, a time of inspiration and encouragement.

May we find it to be challenging, a time of rededication and renewal.

And may this experience of Advent begin this very moment.

—Source unknown

Last-Minute Gifts

Keep a promise.

Keep a secret.

Share a dream.

Let someone have the last word.

Return a smile.

Let someone in line in front of you.

Listen to a child.

Listen to a senior adult.

Say something nice to someone you like.

Say something nice to someone you don't like.

—Source unknown

That's Love

It's a cruel and ugly world. It always has been. So what does that have to do with Christmas? A lot. It tells you where to look for love—in a stinky food trough where a tiny infant squirms on stale hay 2,000 years ago. Entombed within the tender flesh of that tiny baby was the God of the universe, making the ultimate sacrifice to reconcile men to himself. That's love. And that's the source of a merry Christmas.[6]   —Chuck Swindoll

The Sound of the Christmas Bells

> *There are sounds in the sky when the year grows old,*
> *And the winds of the winter blow—*
> *When night and the moon are clear and cold,*
> *and the stars shine in the snow,*
> *Or wild is the blast and the bitter sleet*
> *That bleats on the window pane;*
> *But blest on the frost hills are the feet*
> *Of the Christmas time again!*
> *Chiming sweet when the night winds swells,*
> *Blest is the sound of the Christmas bells!*

—Anonymous

Baptism

Humor

Baptism Practice

After the baptism of their young boy, the pastor commented to the parents, "I was expecting a few problems. But that boy of yours certainly went through baptism with flying colors!"

The parents replied, "Well, pastor, that's because we've been practicing him. Once a week, my husband has been dunking him in a fish pond." —Source unknown

Call Me Bubba

A minister was baptizing a five-year-old boy. When he announced his name, "Roger Edward the Second," the little boy interrupted, "Mister, I'm a third not a second, and if it's all right with you, I'd rather be called 'Bubba.'" —Source unknown

Cat Baptism

The four-year-old daughter of a preacher was conducting a "baptism" in the backyard. She picked up a cat and held it over a rain barrel.

Trying to mimic her father, she placed the cat in the barrel and said, "I baptize you in the name of the Father, the Son, and in the hole-you-go."   —Charles Foster[7]

Immersed or Sprinkled?

A Presbyterian and a Baptist minister were having an intense discussion about baptism. The Baptist minister insisted that the candidates should be fully immersed, while the Presbyterian minister opted for sprinkling. The Presbyterian minister asked some qualifying questions.

"Is he baptized if he is in water up to his chin?"

"No," the Baptist minister replied.

"Up to his nose?" asked the Presbyterian.

Again the response, "No."

"How about up to his eyebrows?"

"No," the Baptist minister insisted.

"His eyebrows?"

"No," the Baptist minister responded, "he must have his whole head under water!"

"See," the Presbyterian minister added, "it's the water on top of his head that counts!"[8]

More Water, Please

The pastor guided the young candidate into the baptismal pool. "Your full name," the pastor asked.

"Edward Jeffrey Charles Martin Mackenzie the Third," the boy loudly announced.

The custodian shouted, "Hold it, Preacher! I'll go get some more water!"[9]

The Church Mouse Problem

At a conference of church custodians, there was a discussion about getting rid of mice. Several solutions were offered.

One custodian said, "We put out some mousetraps with the finest cheese in town in them, but it didn't help. About a week later, they came right back."

Another custodian responded, "We locked a cat in the church at night. For several months, we didn't have a mouse problem. But eventually they came back."

"How did you solve the problem?" they asked a third custodian.

"Easy. We put 'em in a membership class, then six weeks later, the pastor baptized them. That was ten years ago. Haven't seen 'em since!"[10]

The Lutheran Pastor's First Baptism

The new pastor at the Lutheran church asked the pastor at First Baptist Church if he could use the baptismal tank. Three people from the Lutheran church had requested baptism by immersion.

The Lutheran pastor was unfamiliar with the ceremony, so he asked the host pastor for some tips. "I make a few comments," the pastor offered, "and then, I carefully bend the person back under the water."

The preliminaries went well, but there was a problem when the baptisms began. The Lutheran minister put the candidates under the water first—and made his lengthy comments while they were there. A loud gasp was heard when each candidate surfaced.

—Barry Kolamowski[11]

We'll Loan You the Tub

The minister of a different denomination contacted the pastor of a large Baptist church and made an unusual request. He had several folks who had recently joined his church who preferred to be baptized by immersion rather than sprinkling, the church's normal mode of baptism. The minister requested the use of their baptistry *and* the Baptist pastor himself. This posed a dilemma—what if those being baptized weren't born again? Wishing to handle his answer with tact, he wrote the pastor, "We don't take in laundry, but we'll be happy to loan you our tub?"

—Charles R. Swindoll[12]

Illustrations

Baptism Is like a Wedding Ring

Baptism is like a wedding ring: they both symbolize transactions. A wedding ring symbolizes marriage, just as baptism symbolizes salvation. Wearing a wedding ring does not make you married any more than being baptized makes you saved.

—The Autoillustrator Online[13]

I Would Give My Life

The great pianist Paderewski finished his performance and was greeted by one of his fans. "I would give my life to play the piano like that!"

Paderewski responded, "I have done just that, Sir."

—Source unknown

Painful Silence

It is said that when St. Patrick baptized King Aengus in the fifth century, he accidentally stabbed the king's foot with his pointed staff. Following the baptism, St. Patrick noticed blood on the water and realized what he did.

"Sire, why did you suffer such pain in silence?" he asked.

The king answered, "I thought it was part of the baptism."

—sermonillustrations.com[14]

The Baptism of Charles Haddon Spurgeon

Charles Haddon Spurgeon was reared in a Congregational home. Both his father and grandfather were preachers. He was baptized on his mother's birthday, and the water and weather were so cold that a fire was built by the people standing on the banks so they could keep warm. Spurgeon, then 16, had walked eight miles that morning to be baptized.

Later, he not only preached to great throngs in London's 5,000-seat Metropolitan Tabernacle, but for 40 years in England, Europe, and America, his sermons sold 150 million copies. In addition, he wrote 135 books that were translated into many languages. —J. B. Fowler Jr.[15]

The Narrow Road

A missionary was trying to explain what it means to follow Christ. "The Christian life is like walking a narrow road."

His student replied with wisdom beyond his years, "Yes, a narrow road. There is only room for one, Christ in me."

—Source unknown

Too Much Baptism

Concerned that the preacher was preaching on the subject of baptism too regularly, the deacons suggested he change subjects.

"Give me another subject, then, and I'll give it a try," the preacher responded.

They suggested Gen. 1.

The next Sunday, the preacher began his message, "I've been requested to preach from Genesis 1. I like that because it suggests that when the Lord created our planet, He made most of it water, and that sorta reminds me of baptism." —Roy B. Zuck[16]

Where Are the Lamps?

A nobleman built a church for the residents of a tiny village in Europe. Since no one was allowed into the church until its completion, the grateful residents wondered what it would look like.

On the day of dedication, worshippers surveyed their new church.

"Where are the lamps?" one of the members asked.

"There aren't any lamps," the nobleman replied. "There are only hooks on the wall. You must bring your own lamp."

"I'm curious, Sir," another member asked, "why must we bring our own lamps?"

The benefactor answered, "It's a reminder that when you are not here, that area of the church will be without light."

—Source unknown

Quotes

Baptism in India

A part of the act of baptism (for new members, not the ordination of ministers) in the Church of India is for the candidate to place his own hand on his head and say, "Woe is me if I preach not the gospel."   —E. Paul Hovey[17]

Baptism Defined

Baptism is the declaration of the universal face of the sonship of man to God.   —Phillips Brooks

Baptism Signified

Baptism signifies that the old Adam in us is to be drowned by daily sorrow and repentance, and perish with all sins and evil lusts; and that the new man should daily come forth again and rise, who shall live before God in righteousness and purity forever.

—*Luther's Small Catechism*[18]

Book of Common Prayer

Being by nature born in sin, and the children of wrath, we are hereby made the children of grace.

—*Book of Common Prayer: The Catechism*

Baptism, the Direction

In baptism, the Christian is born. His old self is buried and the new self emerges . . . The direction is indicated rather than the arrival.   —Friedrich Rest[19]

Baptism Community

The person being baptized experiences the firm support of the community—of the Body of Christ—in the arms and hands of the minister, feels the plunge of commitment, and bursts into new life with the sound and feel of rushing water.   —Source unknown

Die to Self

We may never be martyrs but we can die to self, to sin, to the world, to our plans and ambitions. That is the significance of baptism; we died with Christ and rose to a new life. —Vance Havner[20]

Christmas

Humor

Christmas Preacher

A four-year-old recited her version of a holiday favorite, "'Twas the night before Christmas and all through the house, not a *preacher* was stirring, not even a mouse." —Perry Greene

Good All the Time

Asked why she said she liked Santa better than Jesus, a little girl replied, "You only have to be good at Christmas for Santa. But for Jesus . . . well, you have to be good for Him all the time." —Vance Havner[21]

'Twas the Night Before

> *'Twas the night before Christmas and all through the house,*
> *Not a creature was stirring 'cept Dad and his spouse.*
> *Their faces were haggard, all wrinkled with care.*
> *They looked at each other and sighed with despair.*
> *Could they both be enjoying the presents they got?*
> *From the look on their faces, we knew they were not.*
> *It was simple to us what was causing their ills.*
> *They were figuring out how to pay all the bills.*
>
> —Source unknown

Is Santa Claus Real?

Little five-year-old Victoria seemed more subdued than normal as her father drove her to school. Her father, Fred, said, "You seem deep in thought. What are you thinking about?"

Victoria replied, "I'm thinking about the Easter bunny."

"Oh really," said Fred, "and what are you thinking about the Easter bunny?" he probed.

She said, "Well . . . he's not real!"

Fred thought this might be a teachable moment—one of those moments when the distinction between fantasy and reality is made clear. So he pressed Victoria with another question. "And what about Santa Claus?" he inquired.

Victoria replied, "Oh . . . Santa doesn't think the Easter bunny is real, either."

—Stan Toler

Look Inside

The little neighbor boy got a trumpet for Christmas. His loud playing bothered the elderly gentleman next door, until one day he stopped the boy outside. "What do you call that beautiful instrument I hear you playing?"

"It's a trumpet," the boy replied.

"What's inside that thing that makes it sound so lovely?"

"I don't know," the boy answered.

The neighbor pulled out a screwdriver and a set of pliers, "Here, take these and look inside."

—Source unknown

Synchronized Shopping

A family went Christmas shopping at the mall. Outside the entrance, Dad assembled Mom and the kids.

"We'll meet back here in two hours," Dad announced. "So, let's synchronize our watches."

Mom tapped Dad on the shoulder, "I think we ought to synchronize our credit cards too."

—Source unknown

The Clean Wise Men

The five-year-old broke into the family Christmas carol sing, "I'm glad those wise men were nuts about being clean!"

"Why do you say that?" Dad asked.

The boy replied, "The song says the shepherds washed their socks by night."

—Source unknown

The Other Person in the Plane

A Sunday School teacher asked her students to draw a picture of the Bethlehem family. The drawing of one student surprised her: Mary, Joseph, and Baby Jesus were pictured riding in an airplane. The teacher inquired, "That's an interesting picture, Jimmy, but who's that other person in the plane?"

The little boy replied, "That's Pontius. He's the pilot."

—Source unknown

Three Wise Women?

Ever wonder what would have happened if it had been three wise women instead of three wise men? They would have asked directions, arrived on time, helped deliver the baby, cleaned up the stable, made a casserole, and brought practical gifts.

—E-mail from Jeanne Griffin

Wrong Card!

Getting a late start on the holidays, a lady hurriedly bought a box of identical Christmas cards from the sale table at the corner pharmacy.

With the post office mail deadline quickly approaching, she quickly signed, addressed, stamped, and mailed the cards to 75 of her friends and relatives.

A few days later, her best friend called. "Sarah, I thought we agreed not to exchange gifts this year?"

"We did," Sarah replied. "I only sent you a card, just like we agreed."

"Did you read it?" her friend asked.

"I don't think so," she replied. "What did your card say?"

She read the message, "Just a note to say, a Christmas gift is on the way!"

—Stan Toler

Illustrations

An Unforgettable Christmas

Christmas Day, 1961, will always be a memorable day for the Toler family. Winter had been long and hard with lots of snow and cold weather. Times were tough! Dad was laid off from construction work, our food supply dwindled to nothing, and we closed off most of the house due to our inability to afford high utility bills.

On Christmas Eve, Mom noted we would have no food Christmas Day. She suggested that we accept a handout from the government Commodity Department. So Dad loaded Terry and me into his old Plymouth and we headed downtown. That evening we stood in line with others for what seemed like hours, waiting on the government handouts—cheese, dried milk, flour, and dried eggs.

Finally, Dad could stand it no longer. "We're going home, boys," he said. "God will provide!" We cried, but completely trusted Dad's faith in God.

That night, we popped popcorn and opened the gifts we had ordered with Mom's Top Value Trading Stamps, saved for Christmas presents. Terry ordered a transistor radio, I ordered a Brownie Kodak camera, and Mark got a baby toy. We were so grateful to have anything!

Everyone slept well under Grandma's handmade quilts that night. We were just happy to be together as a family.

On Christmas Day morning, December 25, 1961, we were startled by a loud knock and Merry Christmas greetings from people who attended our church. They arrived with gifts, clothing, and a 30-day supply of food. Since that day, I have always believed that "God will provide" and that whenever there is need, He has a pre-arranged supply to meet the need through His people.

—Stan Toler

Greater than a Walk on the Moon

Charles L. Allen said that he lived around the block from one of the astronauts who walked on the moon. Commenting on the thrill of living near one who had a part in that historic event, Allen added, "The greatest event in human history was not when a human being walked on the moon. The greatest event in human history was when God became a man."

—*The Vance Havner Quote Book*[22]

I've Wanted One of These

After ripping into a Christmas present, a three-year-old girl picked up the toy and said, "Ooohhh, I've wanted one of these ever since I was a little girl."

The marvelous thing about the joy of Christmas is that we didn't know we wanted it until it came. And the minute we first beheld God's glory wrapped in swaddling clothes, we knew it was what we had always wanted; what we had always needed. It fills us with joy. —*The Abingdon Preaching Manual, 1966*

Origin of Some Christmas Traditions

- The Christmas tree began as a German tradition as early as A.D. 700 and moved to England and America through immigrants.
- The first manufactured Christmas tree ornament was sold at Woolworths in 1880. Martin Luther is credited with first decorating trees with candles in the 16th century. Calvin Coolidge ceremoniously lit the first outdoor tree at the White House in 1923.
- Mistletoe has been used as a decoration for thousands of years, but because of its association with pagan rituals, the Church forbade its use in any form, suggesting holly as a substitute. The pointed leaves of the holly were to symbolize the thorns on Christ's crown and the red berries, the drops of His blood.
- Christmas cards started in London in 1843, and in America in 1848. Today, about 2 billion Christmas cards are exchanged each year in the United States.[23]

The Christmas Message

On Christmas Eve, the headmaster of a children's home was preparing his Christmas message. A dorm mother knocked on the door and explained that one of the children was upset because he didn't get to go home for Christmas.

Following her to the boy's room, the headmaster discovered the troubled boy under his bed. Standing next to the bed, he tried to converse with him but there was no response.

Finally, he dropped to his knees and lifted the bedspread. Tear-stained eyes looked out. Instead of forcefully pulling the boy out, he dropped to the floor, crawled under the bed, and held out his hand.

The boy placed his tiny hand into the hand of the headmaster. The headmaster had his Christmas message. God stooped to the earth and gave us Jesus. In our fear, loneliness, and sin, He crawled in beside us and held out His hand.   —Henry Carter[24]

The Christmas Wrapping

Frank Meade quotes from the First Baptist Church Bulletin of Syracuse, N.Y. "There was a gift for each of us under the tree of life 2,000 years ago by Him whose birthday we celebrate today. The gift was withheld from no man. Some have left the packages unclaimed. Some have accepted the gift and carry it around, but have failed to remove the wrappings and to look inside to discover hidden splendor. The packages are all alike. In each is a scroll on which is written, "All that the Father has is yours. Take and live!"[25]

The Image of God

A famous fresco in Rome, called *The Aurora*, was painted on the ceiling of a palace! Looking up to see it, you can become dizzy and stiff-necked as the figures become indistinct. After several complaints, the palace owner placed a mirror near the floor. The reflection of the picture becomes clearer and you can sit for hours and contemplate its beauty.

Frank Fairchild observed, "Jesus Christ does precisely that for us when we try to get some notion of God. He is the mirror of Deity—the express image of God's person. In Him, God becomes visible and intelligible to us. We cannot, by any amount of searching, find God. The more we try, the more we are bewildered. Then Jesus Christ appears. He is God stooping down to our level, and He enables our feeble thoughts to get some real hold on God Himself."

—Walter Knight[26]

The Unopened Gift

During their gift exchange, a family noticed a small but beautifully wrapped gift under the tree, near the back. It didn't have a name tag. Who was it from? To whom was it intended? Was it a gift that someone wanted but didn't receive? There were a lot of questions, as they passed the gift around and tried to guess its contents.

It made such an impact on the family that they made it a tradition to leave one unopened gift under the Christmas tree.

—Troy Surratt[27]

What Makes Christmas Perfect?

As a little girl, I thought Christmas was perfect the year I received my shiny green and silver Western Flyer bicycle. I had slipped out of bed on Christmas Eve night to sneak a peek at gifts under the tree. However, I was halted at the door by an eerie, yet wonderful gleam from the living room. Something was reflecting the moonlight from the window. The next morning, I discovered my beautiful bike.

As a young teen, I thought the perfect Christmas was spent at my grandparents' home on Christmas Day. Nanny always made roast turkey with two kinds of dressing, two other meats, and a multitude of fancy delicacies. But now my grandparents are gone. The old farmhouse has been sold. The Christmases at that country farmhouse seemed perfect, but now they are only treasured memories.

As a young adult, I remember the adventure of my first Christmas with my husband, Stan, and his family. We were engaged to be married; life was wonderful. We were in love. It was the perfect Christmas! But, even so, it meant being away from my parents for the first time at Christmas. I remember Mother cried when I gave her a very crude, little clay pitcher I had made in a college art class. I realize now, it couldn't have been the perfect Christmas, if separation and sadness were a part of it.

Now, I think I have a better understanding of what makes the perfect Christmas. It doesn't matter about age, occupation, or social position. All that really counts is the relationship I have with Jesus Christ.

For the perfect Christmas, we must experience Jesus as our Lord and Savior.   —Linda Toler

Where Is Jesus' Present?

Little Olivia was allowed to pass out the Christmas gifts the Christmas Eve she learned to read. According to family custom the one who distributed the presents would be allowed to open the first gift. After all the presents were distributed with care, Linda kept looking around among the branches. Her father asked, "Honey, what are you looking for?"

The little girl replied, "I thought Christmas was Jesus' birthday, and I was just wondering where His present is. I guess everyone forgot Him. Did they, Daddy?"[28]

Quotes

Cut the Cost

Everybody'd be happier this Christmas if we'd just cut the cost and revive the reverence.   —Oren Arnold[29]

Give What You Have

Give what you have. To someone, it may be better than you dare to think.   —Henry Wadsworth Longfellow

Finding Christmas

He who has not Christmas in his heart will never find it under a tree.   —Roy L. Smith[30]

We Can Have Joy

It must be said that we can have joy, and therefore will have it, only as we give it to others.   —Karl Barth

Keep Christmas Within

> *Then let every heart keep its Christmas within*
> *Christ's pity for sorrow, Christ's hatred for sin,*
> *Christ's care for the weakest, Christ's courage for right,*
> *Christ's dread of the darkness, Christ's love of the light.*
> *Everywhere, everywhere, Christmas tonight.*
>   —Phillips Brooks

The Christmas List

> *I had the nicest Christmas list*
> *The longest one in town,*
> *Till Father looked at it and said,*
> *"You'll have to cut it down."*
> *I knew that what he said was true*
> *Beyond the faintest doubt,*
> *But was amazed to hear him say,*
> *"You've left your best Friend out."*
> *And so I scanned my list again*
> *And said, "That's just not true!"*
> *But Father said, "His name's not there,*
> *The Friend who died for you."*
>
> *And then I clearly understood*
> *'Twas Jesus that He meant:*
> *For Him who should come first of all,*
> *I hadn't planned a cent.*

—Source unknown

The Feet of the Humblest

> *The feet of the humblest may walk in the fields*
> *Where the feet of the holiest have trod.*
> *This is the marvel to mortals revealed,*
> *When the silvery trumpets of Christmas have pealed,*
> *That mankind are the children of God.*

—Phillips Brooks

No Room

That there was no room in the inn was symbolic of what was to happen to Jesus. The only place there was room for Him was on the Cross.   —William Barclay

Ordinary Life

When the message was first given it was given not to religious priests, but to shepherds, men of action who were fulfilling their ordinary duties. This put the message into the stream of ordinary life.   —E. Stanley Jones

Commissioning Service

Illustrations

A Cause Worthy of Suffering

Thoreau was jailed for taking part in a protest.

His friend visited him. "What are you doing in jail?" the friend asked.

Thoreau gave a surprising response, "What are you doing out of jail?"   —Source unknown

He Didn't Leave

Max Lucado writes of the night the disciples caught more fish than they could haul into the boat. In the narrative, Peter reflects on the occasion and of his calling, "I don't know what He saw in me, but He didn't leave. Maybe He thought if I would let Him tell me how to fish, I would let Him tell me how to live."

—Max Lucado[31]

Looking for a Chance to Die for Jesus

Missionary C. T. Studd was willing to risk anything and go anywhere for the Lord. When he planned a return to Africa for missionary work, he was warned that he might be killed.

Studd answered, "Praise God, I've been looking for a chance to die for Jesus!"   —John C. Maxwell[32]

Speak About Carey's Savior

Cobbler turned missionary William Carey was a man of great accomplishments. Before his death, he was being considered a missionary hero.

Resisting the lure of missionary fame, his motto was, "The less said about me, the better." And, as he lay dying, he summoned a missionary friend whom he knew would be assisting with his funeral.

He implored, "When I am gone, say nothing about William Carey—speak about Carey's Savior."   —Denise George[33]

The Lord Sends It

Mother Teresa was asked if there was enough money to complete a welfare project. She replied, "Money—I don't think about it. It always comes. The Lord sends it. We do His work. He provides the means. If He does not give us the means, that shows He does not want the work." —Kathryn Spink[34]

Quotes

Do Our Part

God will not do what people can do, He expects us to do our part. People cannot do what God can do, only God can do His part.

—Elmer Towns

Qualified

Often, God doesn't call the qualified. But always, He qualifies the called. —Source unknown

What God Chooses

What God chooses, He cleanses.
What God cleanses, He molds.
What God molds, He fills.
What God fills, He uses.

—J. S. Baxter[35]

Communion

Humor

First Communion

A three-year-old took her first Communion. The pastor patted her on the head as he gave her the elements, "God be with you."

When she got home she pretended to serve Communion to her dolls. Her mother watched as she passed pieces of bread to each of the dolls, patted them on the head and said softly, "God will get you." —Source unknown

They Didn't Give Him Much

One weekend my little brother was visiting our grandparents in another town. They took him to church with them, and on Sunday after church, he asked what Communion was all about.

Granddad replied, "That was Jesus' last supper."

My little brother replied, "Boy, they didn't give Him much, did they?"   —Elaine Borcber[36]

Illustrations

A Trophy of Friendship

A wounded World War II soldier was brought to the field hospital clutching the helmet of a German soldier.

"I see you have a trophy of the kill," the army nurse commented.

The soldier responded, "No, Ma'am. It's a trophy of friendship."

He then explained, "An enemy soldier and I both lay wounded on the battlefield. I crawled over to him and bound his wounds; and he did the same for me. We couldn't understand each other's languages, so I thanked him by giving him my helmet, and he thanked me by giving his helmet to me."

The soldier continued, "And then we both suffered together in silence until the medics came."   —*The Christian Herald*

Communion Kindness

A Sunday School teacher knelt beside the nine-year-old at the Communion rail. She sensed the boy's nervousness as he handled the chrome tray of tiny glasses. As he took one of the glasses, he accidentally brushed the tray, spilling its contents on the altar.

With kindness and grace, the Sunday School teacher quickly took out her embroidered handkerchief and wiped the pool of grape juice. She then poured the contents of her cup into the boy's cup, and continued as if nothing had happened.

—George Lyons[37]

Communion Service like a Boy Scout Campfire Meal

The elements of a Boy Scout campfire meal might be instructive for leading an effective Communion service. A wise pastor will attempt to approximate this model.

Boy Scouts: (1) Excitedly anticipate the meal; (2) Almost push and crowd in order to satiate their hunger; (3) Gratefully thank those who make the arrangements; (4) Eat in a spirit of relaxed camaraderie; and (5) Cherish vivid memories about both the adequacy of nourishment and pleasure of the meal.　—Jerry Hull[38]

Imaginary Communion

In the book *Visions of a World Hungry,* Thomas G. Pettepiece tells of being held as a political prisoner. On Easter Sunday, many of his fellow prisoners wanted to participate in a Communion service.

Placing imaginary bread in the empty hands of the prisoners, he said, "Take, eat, this is my body which is given for you; do this in remembrance of me." With bowed heads, the prisoners pretended to put the "bread" into their mouths.

From his empty palm, he then took the "cup" and placed it into their hands, one by one. "Take, drink, this is the blood of Christ which was shed for you. Let us give thanks, knowing that Christ is in this very room."

After they "drank" the "cup" they sang a song of praise, embraced, and went back to their prison cell.

—Thomas G. Pettepiece[39]

The "Gallows Meal"

I discovered something about the Last Supper recently that I had not fully comprehended before. I was watching Stanley Kubrick's classic film *Paths of Glory* on late television. I was deeply struck by the scene of the "gallows meal," the final meal the prisoners shared before their execution. And I realized that the Last Supper was that type of meal: a very emotional occasion, when all superficiality is put aside, when only the most meaningful and honest things are said and done.　—William Toohey[40]

Dedications

Humor

Please Use Other Door

A sign over one of the front doors of a church read, THIS IS THE
ENTRANCE TO HEAVEN. A small sign underneath said, "Please
use other door."   —Source unknown

The Long-winded Dedication Day Speaker

A local church wanted to build a new sanctuary. Among the few
members was a successful contractor who agreed to build the sanctuary *absolutely free* if the church met two conditions: They would
build it as he saw fit, and they wouldn't allow anyone to enter the
building until the day of its dedication.

The board agreed and construction began. Dedication Sunday
arrived and the board was thrilled to see inside their new facility.
They were alarmed, however, because there was only one row of
pews. Then they thought, "What a great idea! Now everyone will
have to sit near the front!"

The speaker spoke far too long. The church board fidgeted.

Suddenly, the contractor stood up and walked to the back of
the church. He pushed a button on a control panel and to everyone's surprise, the pulpit, along with the long-winded speaker,
slowly descended into the basement.

—Stan Toler and Elmer Towns[41]

Illustrations

A Prayer for the Home Dedication

> *God's mercy spread the sheltering roof,*
>   *Let faith make firm the floor;*
> *May friend and stranger, all who come,*
>   *Find love within the door.*
> *May peace enfold each sleeping place,*
>   *And health surround the board;*
> *From all the lamps that light the halls,*

Be radiant joy outpoured.
Let kindness keep the hearth aglow,
And through the windows shine;
Be Christlike living, on the walls,
The pattern and design.

—T. L. Paine[42]

Easter

Humor

Definitions of Easter

A second grade Sunday School class was asked to write out their definitions of Easter.

One wrote: "It's when you get some eggs, a new dress, and you remember God."

Another defined it, "I believe it is the day that God woke up."

But the third student was on target: "It's when Jesus got alive."

—King Duncan and Angela Akers[43]

Easter Plants

During the Sunday morning children's sermon, the pastor asked the young parishioners if they knew what plant was used to symbolize Easter.

A little boy raised his hand, "Pastor, I'm not real sure, but I think it's an eggplant."   —King Duncan and Angela Akers[44]

That Same Hymn

A parishioner shook hands with her pastor after the service and commended him on his sermon.

"I have one small complaint," she added.

"And what's that?" the pastor replied.

"Well, every time I come to this church, they always sing the same hymn!"

"Which one is that?" the pastor inquired.

She replied agitated, "Christ the Lord Is Risen Today!"

—King Duncan[45]

What Did She Get for Easter?

Grandfather asked his granddaughter what her neighbor friend got for Easter.

"Grandpa!" she replied, "she didn't get anything! She's Jewish."

She added, "It's like this, Grandpa: I'm Christmas, and she's Hanukkah. I'm Easter, and she's Passover."

Grandpa replied, "Thank you, honey, that clears it up for me."

"Oh, I forgot one other thing, Grandpa," the granddaughter said.

"What's that?"

She answered with a smile, "Praise the Lord, we're both Halloween!"   —Buddy Westbrook[46]

Illustrations

Beyond the Cross

"The Stations of the Cross" is a tourist attraction in the Italian Alps. Visitors climb a mountain to stand beside an outdoor crucifix. One tourist noticed a trail that led beyond that cross. Fighting rough thicket, she made her way down the small trail. She was surprised to find another shrine. Brush had nearly covered it. It was neglected because visitors had only gone as far as the cross.

Too many have stopped at the cross. They haven't moved beyond its despair and heartbreak to find the real message of Easter: the empty tomb.   —Lavon Brown[47]

Distinguishing the Spiritual from the Ritual

A very small and very devout boy was heard murmuring to himself on Easter morning a poem of his own composition, which began, "Chocolate eggs and Jesus risen." This seems to me, for his age, both admirable poetry and admirable piety.

But, of course, the time will soon come when such a child can no longer effortlessly and spontaneously enjoy that unity. He will become able to distinguish the spiritual from the ritual and festal aspect of Easter; chocolate eggs will no longer be sacramental. And, once he has distinguished, he must put one or the other first. If he puts the spiritual first, he can still taste something of Easter in the chocolate eggs; if he puts the eggs first, they will soon be no more than any other sweetmeat. They have taken on an independent, and therefore a soon-withering, life.   —C. S. Lewis[48]

He Took the Sting

A little boy and his father were playing catch. Suddenly a honeybee swarmed over the boy. The father reacted quickly. His son was highly allergic to bee stings. One sting could prove fatal.

The boy cried out as the father grabbed for the honeybee and caught it in his hand. Then he let it go.

"Dad!" the boy protested. "Why did you let it go?"

His father replied, "It's harmless now."

"How do you know?" the son asked.

"Look here, Son," the father pointed to his hand, "I took the sting. The stinger is still in my hand."   —James Hewett[49]

The Crown of Life

Crowns have always been the sign of authority and royalty. Richard the Lionheart had a crown so heavy that two earls had to stand, one on either side, to hold his head. Edward II once owned nine crowns. The crown that Queen Elizabeth wears is worth over $20 million.

All of them are but trinkets compared to Christ's crown. It was not formed by skilled craftsmen. It was put together hurriedly by the rough hands of Roman soldiers. I deserved to wear it. He took my crown of thorns and offered to me instead His crown of life.

—James Hewett[50]

The Presence of a Risen Christ

A Lutheran bishop in Hungary was imprisoned six years for protesting the confiscating of church schools by the Communist regime.

"They placed me in solitary confinement," he told a Minneapolis assembly. "It was a tiny cell, perhaps six feet by eight feet, with no windows, and soundproofed."

He added, "They hoped to break down my resistance by isolating me from all sensory perceptions. They thought I was alone.

They were wrong. The risen Christ was present in that room, and in communion with Him, I was able to prevail."

—Andrew Wyermann[51]

Quotes

The Lord Laughs Out Loud

Easter is the morning when the Lord laughs out loud, laughs at all the things that snuff out joy, all the things that pretend to be all-powerful, like cruelty and madness and despair and evil, and most especially, that great pretender, death.   —Frank Yates[52]

New Year's Day of the Soul

Easter is the New Year's Day of the soul.   —A. B. Simpson[53]

Contemplate Death

I don't know anybody who can contemplate his own death and hum a tune at the same time.   —Woody Allen[54]

Love's Redeeming Work Is Done

> Love's redeeming work is done.
> Fought the fight, the battle won.
> Death in vain forbids him rise
> Christ has opened paradise.

—Charles Wesley

New Here and Now

The great Easter truth is not that we are to live newly after death—that is not the great thing—but that we are to be new here and now by the power of the Resurrection.   —Phillips Brooks[55]

Easter Without Good Friday

Observing Easter without Good Friday teaches a half-truth.

—Keith Drury

Our Enemies Are Beaten

The Easter message tells us that our enemies—sin, the curse, and death—are beaten. Ultimately they can no longer start mischief. They still behave as though the game was not decided, the battle not fought; we must still reckon with them, but fundamentally we must cease to fear them anymore.   —Karl Barth[56]

Resurrection in Every Leaf

Our Lord has written the promise of resurrection, not in books alone, but in every leaf of springtime.   —Martin Luther

Rock of Ages

The heavy, ponderous stone that sealed Jesus in the confines of that rock-walled tomb was but a pebble compared to the Rock of Ages inside.   —James Hewett[57]

Resurrection Experience

The resurrection never becomes a fact of experience until the risen Lord lives in the heart of the believer.   —Peter Marshall[58]

Father's Day

Humor

God Created All This

A father was trying to explain the Creation to his son as they walked through the woods, "Son, God made all of this—every single leaf, on every single tree."

"Yeah, I know, Dad," the boy responded excitedly. "And He did it all with His left hand!"

"With His left hand?" the father asked. "Where did you ever hear that?"

"Last Sunday, my Sunday School teacher read from the Bible, and it said that Jesus was sitting on His Father's right hand."

—Source unknown

How Old Is Daddy?

Sitting around the dinner table, the discussion turned to Daddy's age. "I know how old he is!" the youngest member of the family announced.

"How old do you think he is?" Mom asked.

"He's 40," the little brother replied.

"And how do you know that?" his mother asked.

Stirring the vegetables on his plate, he answered, "Mom, remember when you were folding clothes the other day? Well, his age was on his underwear."   —Stan Toler

Looks Aren't Everything

Looking very solemn, the doctor motioned for the wife of his patient to meet him outside the examining room.

"I'll have to say, your husband just doesn't look good to me."

"Me either," she responded. "But looks aren't everything. And besides that, he's a good father."[59]

Put Away Childish Things

Dad came home from work and tried to put the car in the garage. Before he could get to the garage he had to clean out the driveway. First, he put the bike aside; then the basketball; next the inline skates; then the baseball bat; and then the remote control race car.

Greeting his wife at the door, he said, "You know, Honey, now I know what that Scripture verse means, 'When I became a man, I put away childish things.'"[60]

The Bible Story Question

A father was reading a Bible story to his young son. Reading about God's warning to Lot to flee the city and not turn back, he was suddenly interrupted, "Dad, whatever happened to the flea?"

—Source unknown

The Cost Is Worth It

Two fathers were discussing the cost of raising children. "I know the costs are great, but it's worth it to me just to have someone in the house who knows how to operate our computer."

—Jerry Brecheisen

What Does Dad Have to Do with It?

Two daughters were having a discussion about family resemblance. "I look like Mom," said my nine-year-old, "but I have Dad's eyes and Dad's lips."

The six-year-old said, "And I look just like Dad, but I have light hair." Then she turned to me. "Mom," she asked, "what does Dad have to do with us being born anyway?"

Her older sister jumped right in. "Don't be stupid, Christina. Dad is the one who drove Mom to the hospital."

—Kathleen O'Neill[61]

When You Grow Up

"Son, what will you be doing when you grow up and become as big as your father?" a father asked philosophically.

His little boy replied quickly, "Dieting!"

—Mark Hollingsworth

Illustrations

Look for the Gold

Andrew Carnegie on developing people: "You develop people in the same way you mine for gold. When you mine for gold, you move tons of dirt to find a single ounce of gold. However, you don't look for the dirt—you look for the gold."[62]

Only One Thing Mattered

Entering the parsonage at the end of a full and hectic Sunday, the phone rang. It was a disgruntled church member calling to register a complaint about the building program. For the next 30 minutes she took me to task on every facet of ministry.

Upstairs, my wife was giving our 18-month-old son his evening bath. As the lady droned on, I heard my wife, "Seth Aaron Toler, come back here!"

Naked and sliding down the stairs head first, he was soon in my lap. Bath water covered my suit as he shivered and shook his curly blond head. He hugged me, and kissed me on each cheek. "Daddy," he said, "I wuv you!"

Tears streamed down my cheeks, as the caller finalized her Sunday evening "fireside" chat. In that moment, only one thing mattered. I knew I was loved. God was not late when I needed encouragement!   —Stan Toler

The Safest Place to Stand

Max Lucado tells of speaking at a funeral of a family friend. The friend's son told of an incident when a tornado hit their small town.

His father hustled the kids indoors and had them lie under a mattress. The son remembered peeking out from under the mattress and seeing his father standing by a window, watching the funnel cloud.

When the young boy saw his father, he crawled out from under the mattress, and ran to rap his arms around his dad's leg.

"Something told me," he said, "that the safest place to stand in a storm was next to my father."[63]

You Didn't Ask Your Dad to Help

A little boy struggled with a big rock that someone had mischievously placed in his sandbox. Since it stood in the way of the "freeway" that he was constructing in the sand, it had to be removed.

He dug around the rock and loosened it. He tried to lift it but he couldn't. He lay down in the sand and tried to push it with his feet. It wouldn't budge.

The little boy's dad noticed the effort and came over to the sandbox. "What's the problem, Son?"

"Daddy, I've tried everything to get this big rock out of the sandbox," the boy replied tearfully.

"No, I'm afraid you haven't tried everything."

"What do you mean, Daddy?"

The dad reached down and picked up the rock, "You didn't ask your dad to help." —Wayne Rice[64]

Quotes

Until He Becomes a Father

A man never knows how to be a son until he becomes a father . . . By the time a man realizes that maybe his father was right, he usually has a son who thinks he's wrong. —Source unknown

God's Character

If God's character is to be understood in terms of my life [as a father], what does my child think of God? —Lee Haines[65]

Build Boys

It is easier to build boys than to mend men.[66]

Correct the Example

One of the best ways to correct your children is to correct the example you are setting for them. —Source unknown

Successful Family

While I don't minimize the vital role played by a mother, I believe a successful family begins with her husband. —James Dobson[67]

Funeral

Illustrations

Golf Stroke Honors a Friend

Golfer Payne Stewart died tragically in an airplane crash. In the last five years of his life, he had made a deep commitment to Christ, and his faith was well known in golfing circles.

A fellow Christian golfer memorialized his friend at the next professional golf tournament in Houston. Instead of taking his driver to the first tee, golfer Bob Estes took his putter. Standing over the ball for a few moments, he then putted it about 15 feet.

"That's for Payne," he announced quietly. In a game where each stroke could be worth thousands, Estes voluntarily gave up a stroke in honor of a man who considered his faith and his family more important than a golf score.[68]

Hit by a Shadow

When Donald Barnhouse's wife died, he was left with young daughters to raise alone. While driving to that funeral, which he conducted himself, he wanted to say something to explain all of this to his girls.

They stopped at a traffic light. It was a bright day, and the sun streamed into the car. A truck pulled up next to them, and its shadow darkened the inside of the car. He turned to them and asked whether they would prefer to be hit by the truck or its shadow. They answered: "The shadow can't hurt you."

Quoting Psalm 23, "Even though I walk through the valley of the shadow of death, I will fear no evil, for you are with me," he explained that their mother's death was as if she had been hit by a shadow. It was as if Jesus had stepped in the way in her place.

—Leith Anderson[69]

I Know Where He Is

Trying to explain the sudden death of her grandpa to her little girl, her mother said, "Honey, Grandpa has gone to live with Jesus."

Later, the granddaughter overheard her mother talking on the phone about Grandpa's death, "I lost my father several months ago."

After she hung up the phone, the little girl spoke up, "Mommy, we didn't lose Grandpa. I know where he is."[70]

Let's Make Something Out of the Pieces

A father and son were building a model airplane. Suddenly, the family pet raced through the room and brushed against the small table they were working on. The near-finished model crashed to the floor.

The boy began to cry. "It's gone! It's gone! Dad, we worked so hard on that model, and now it's gone!"

The father wisely cradled his son in his arms and said, "It's not all gone, Son. There are some pieces left. Let's pick them up and make something out of them."[71]

One Thing for Sure

A new mother heard about a wise old man in a nearby Greek village. Seeking counsel on raising her child, she asked the man about the child's future.

"There is one thing I can tell you for sure about your child."

Excitedly, the mother asked, "Oh, what is that?"

The man laid his hand on her shoulder and replied solemnly, "Someday your child will die. There is no exception."

—Leith Anderson[72]

She Turned to a Nazarene Carpenter

At a prayer breakfast, then Vice President George H. W. Bush told of a trip to Russia. He was there to represent the United States at the funeral of Leonid Brezhnev. He said the funeral was precise and stoic. No tears were shed and no emotion was shown.

There was one exception. Mrs. Brezhnev was the last to witness the body before the coffin was closed. She stood by its side for a few moments, and then reached down to perform the sign of the cross on her husband's chest.

In the hour of death, she went not to Lenin, not to Karl Marx, not to Krushchev. She turned to a Nazarene carpenter who had lived two thousand years ago and who dared to claim: "Don't let your hearts be troubled. Trust in God, and trust in me."

—Max Lucado[73]

Quotes

Crossing the Bar

> Sunset and evening star,
>   And one clear call for me!
> And may there be no moaning at the bar,
>   When I put out to sea.

But such a tide as moving seems asleep,
*   Too full for sound and foam,*
When that which drew from out the boundless deep,
*   Turns again home.*

Twilight and evening bell,
*   And after that the dark!*
And may there be no sadness of farewell,
*   When I embark.*

For though from out our bourne of Time and Place
*   The flood may bear me far,*
I hope to see my Pilot face to face
*   When I have crossed the bar.*

—Alfred Lord Tennyson

How Long, O Lord?

He who "lives forever" has placed himself at the head of a band of
pilgrims who mutter, "How long, O Lord? How long?"

"How long must I endure this sickness?"

"How long must I endure this spouse?"

"How long must I endure this paycheck?"

Do you really want God to answer? He could, you know. He
could answer in terms of the here and now with time increments
we know. "Two more years on the illness." "The rest of your life in
the marriage." "Ten more years for the bills."

But He seldom does that. He usually opts to measure the here
and now against the there and then. And when you compare this
life to that life, this life ain't that long.

—Max Lucado[74]

The Interlude

Death
Is a soft interlude
Between the noises of time
And the solitude of eternity.

Its melody is penned
By the Heavenly Composer,
And performed by earthly
Musicians,
Who play its score
With chords of faith
Or discords of unbelief,
In a somber rehearsal
Of an everlasting
Symphony.

—Jerry Brecheisen

The Tomb Is Not a Blind Alley

The tomb is not a blind alley; it is a thoroughfare. It closes on the twilight to open with the dawn.

—Victor Hugo

This I Know

Grief has its rhythm—first, the
Wild swift tide of dark despair,
The time of bleak aloneness
When even God seems not there.

And then, the slow receding—
Till quiet calms the sea,
And bare, unwashed sand everywhere
Where castles used to be.

The gentle lapping of the waves
Upon the short—and then,
The pearl lined shells of memories
To help us smile again.

—Source unknown

Graduation

Humor

Freshman Dreams

It was Parents' Day at State College. Some of the parents had gathered in the coffee shop. One remarked, "I'm sure you have so many dreams for that freshman son of yours!"

His mother replied, "Yes, of course. For several years now, we've been dreaming of the day he becomes a sophomore."[75]

The Only One with the Answer

Johnny came home from school crying. "What on earth is wrong?" his mother inquired.

"The teacher asked a question in school today, and I was the only one who could answer it," he sobbed.

"Honey, why would that make you sad. I should think you would be proud," his mother remarked. "What was the question?"

Johnny brushed the tears, "Who put the Super Glue on my chair!"   —Mark Hollingsworth

Illustrations

Building a Place in the Heart

William Rockefeller, brother of John D. Rockefeller, announced that he was going to build a tomb for himself that would cost over a quarter of a million dollars.

A writer in *Forbes* magazine commented, "Few men of his wealth and opportunities have more completely failed to build for themselves a worthy place in the hearts of their fellow men."
                                       —David W. Richardson[76]

Planned Neglect

A famed concert pianist was asked how she had become such a virtuoso. She replied, "Planned neglect." Everything else had been sacrificed to meet her goal of being a pianist.[77]

The Same in Any Language

A Christian worker from Argentina was sent to the United States for language training.

Eager to tell others about Christ, and unfamiliar with English, his problem was increased by his assignment to a language class comprised mostly of Japanese students.

One day, a Japanese student in the secular school asked him to tell her about Jesus.

Soon other Japanese students, many of them Buddhists, gathered around. The Argentinian Christian read from his Spanish/English Bible while the students compared the scripture portions in their Japanese/English Bibles. A Bible study began that was continued by other Christians.

The worker returned to his homeland assured that the Word of God was the same in any language.   —Michael R. Estep[78]

One More Class

About the time we're ready to graduate from the school of experience, somebody adds one more class.   —Mark Hollingsworth

I Believe in College

I believe in college because it takes kids away from home at the point when they start asking questions.   —Will Rogers[79]

A Splendid Torch

Life is no brief candle to me. It is a splendid torch which I have got hold of for the moment, and I want to make it burn as brightly as possible before handing it on to future generations.

—George Bernard Shaw

Grandparents Day

Humor

Did I Tell You About My Grandchildren?

A busy executive was working on his laptop computer during a flight.

An elderly lady sat next to him and began to talk unceasingly. The busy man tried to politely listen and continue working at the same time.

Suddenly, the lady started digging through her purse. She asked, "Did I tell you about my grandchildren?"

"No, Ma'am," the executive answered. "And I really appreciate it!"   —Melvin Maxwell

I Can't Remember

The young preacher sensed he was losing his audience to deep sleep. Thinking he would bring them back to life with shock, he announced, "I lived with a woman for 18 years and she wasn't even my wife."

The audience was stunned. But the preacher added, "She wasn't my wife, she was my mother!"

A preacher who had witnessed the tactic decided to use it when he served as the substitute for a pastor in a neighboring church.

"For 18 years, I lived with a woman and she wasn't my wife."

His audience had a similar reaction, but the inexperienced supply preacher suddenly had a memory lapse.

He repeated, "For 18 years, I lived with a woman who wasn't my wife, but I can't remember who she was!"   —Source unknown

Holiness

Quotes

Three Distinctives of Sanctification

1. There is a consciousness of inbred sin and moral deficiency after conversion, and the more devoted and faithful the justified soul, the clearer and stronger this conviction.

2. There is conviction, in the light of gospel provisions, of the duty and privilege of being "cleansed from all sin," and made "pure in heart."

3. It is prayerfully sought and experienced as in instantaneous cleansing by faith in the blood of Christ.

—J. A. Wood[80]

After God's Own Heart

God's heart is a deep mystery; His will is a revelation of that mystery. The man who seeks to do all of God's will is on the way to becoming a man after His heart. —Andrew Murray

Degree of Perfection

God made man in that degree of perfection which was pleasing to His own infinite wisdom and goodness. Sin defaced this divine image; Jesus came to restore it. Sin must have no triumph; and the Redeemer of mankind must have His glory. —Adam Clarke[81]

God Is Ever Ready

God is ever ready, by the power of His Spirit to carry us forward to every degree of life, light, and love necessary to prepare us for an eternal weight of glory. —Adam Clarke[82]

Gifts and Talents

Our gifts and talents should also be turned over to Him. They should be recognized for what they are, God's loan to us.

—A. W. Tozer[83]

As One Who Has Died

The Christian shares with Christ in the cross. The crucified Christ lives in him through the Holy Spirit, and the spirit of the cross inspires him. He lives as one who has died with Christ.

—Andrew Murray[84]

Real Revival

Man-made enthusiasm and emotionalism is superficial and cheap. In real revival emotion is not produced or manipulated by man. It is a response to the unsought, unexpected but powerful working of God's Spirit upon the inner depths of people's souls.

—Wesley Duewel[85]

Purity of Intention

Simplicity and purity are the two wings by which a man is lifted above all earthly things. Simplicity is in the intention—purity in the affection. Simplicity tends to God—purity apprehends and tastes Him.   —Thomas à Kempis[86]

Independence Day

Humor

The Patriotic Service

A family not accustomed to attending church visited a local church on a Fourth of July weekend. The entire service focused on patriotism.

After the call to worship and the invocation, the worship leader led the congregation in singing the national anthem.

At end of the last chorus, the family's four-year-old son suddenly shouted, "Play ball!"[87]

What Flag Is This?

The first grade teacher pointed to the American flag, "What flag is this?"

One of the students replied enthusiastically, "That's our country's flag!"

"And what is the name of our country?" the teacher asked.

The student quickly replied, "'Tis of thee."[88]

Illustrations

The Painting

In 1989, a financial analyst from Philadelphia paid $4.00 for a painting at a sale. He didn't care for the painting but liked the frame.

Taking the picture apart, a copy of the Declaration of Independence, about the size of a business envelope, fell out. Years later, he showed it to a friend who encouraged him to have it appraised.

He discovered that hours after finishing work on the Declaration in 1776, the Continental Congress had delivered a handwritten draft to a printer with orders to distribute copies to several state assemblies, conventions, and army officers for display.

Only 24 of the original printings have survived. The one in the picture frame was in mint condition and was sold at a 1991 auction for $2.4 million.[89]

Quotes

History and Morality

History fails to record a single precedent in which nations subject to moral decay have not passed into political and economic decline. There has been either a spiritual awakening to overcome the moral lapse or a progressive deterioration leading to ultimate national disaster. —Douglas MacArthur[90]

Prayer for the Nations

We pray for all the nations of the earth; that in equity and charity their sure foundations may be established; that in piety and wisdom they may find a true welfare, in obedience to Thee, glory and praise; and that, in all the enlargements of their power, they may be ever the joyful servants of Him to whose holy dominion and kingdom shall be no end. —Rev. Richard S. Storrs[91]

Christ or Chaos

The choice before us is plain: Christ or chaos, conviction or compromise, discipline or disintegration. I am rather tired of hearing about our rights and privileges as American citizens. The time is come—it is now—when we ought to hear about the duties and responsibilities of our citizenship. America's future depends upon her accepting and demonstrating God's government.

—Peter Marshall[92]

The Love of Liberty

Our reliance is in the love of liberty which God has planted in us. Our defense is in the spirit which prized liberty as the heritage of all men, in all lands everywhere. Destroy this spirit and you have planted the seeds of despotism at your own doors. Familiarize yourselves with the chains of bondage and you prepare your own limbs to wear them. Accustomed to trample on the rights of others, you have lost the genius of your own independence and become the fit subjects of the first cunning tyrant who rises among you."   —Abraham Lincoln[93]

With Their Feet on the Ground

With their feet on the ground and their eyes on the stars, grassroots leaders everywhere are busy shaping the next American century around the conviction that liberty is a gift from God, not government. Because they know that one man or woman, fired by an idea and free to pursue his or her dreams, can make history, even while making a profit.   —Gerald R. Ford[94]

Infant Dedication

Humor

Blasting or Blessing?

Mother tried to explain to her small child that their best friend's baby was to be blessed in the morning worship service.

The child fell asleep during the long announcements and awoke suddenly as the pastor was delivering the sermon.

To the embarrassment of his family, the child asked out loud, "Did I miss the blasting?"[95]

Illustration

God's Smiling on Me

A little girl was standing by her parents in the church foyer. Suddenly, she began to twirl around in a sunbeam that shone through the window.

"Look, Mommy!" she said enthusiastically, "God's smiling on me!"   —Gwynne M. Day[96]

A Stranger in the House

Newspapers ran the story of a burglar who broke into a house in an upscale neighborhood and lived in the attic for several years before a family member discovered him. The burglar remained quiet when the family was home. When they left, he cooked his meals in the kitchen, watched TV in the family room, and read in the library. The family didn't realize that someone they didn't know was living with them. —Robert Leslie Holmes[97]

Quotes

A Baby

That which makes the home happier,
Love stronger,
Patience greater,
Hands busier,
Nights longer,
Days shorter,
Purses lighter,
Clothes shabbier,
The past forgotten,
The future brighter.

—Marion Lawrence[98]

Limited Time Only

Caption on advertisement for baby product: YOURS FOR A LIMITED TIME ONLY. —Source unknown

Fresh from God

I love these little people; and it is not a slight thing when they, who are so fresh from God, love us. —Charles Dickens[99]

Not Easy Raising Kids

If it was going to be easy to raise kids, it never would have started with something called "labor."[100]

Marvelous Cry

It's marvelous how the cry of a little baby in the still of the night evokes wonder. Usually you wonder which one of you will get up.[101]

Not Too Young to Teach

> *Think not that he is all too young to teach,*
> *His little heart will like a magnet reach*
> *And touch the truth for which you have no speech.*
>
> —Froebel[102]

Labor Day

Humor

Can't Your Family Get Along?

A factory worker was bragging to his coworkers, "Yes, there is a proud fighting tradition in my family! My great-great-grandfather stood his ground at Bunker Hill. Then Great-grandfather valiantly joined up with the troops to destroy the Germans. My grandfather was at Pearl Harbor. And my father fought the North Koreans."

"Mercy!" one of the coworkers remarked. "Can't your family get along with anyone?"   —Stan Toler

Salary Range?

"What salary range are we looking at?" the Human Resources person asked a young college graduate.

"Oh, I'd say in the neighborhood of about $80,000," he replied.

"What if I doubled that amount?" she asked.

"You must be kidding!" the astonished job applicant remarked.

She replied quickly, "You're right! But don't forget, you started it."[103]

That Day Off

So, you want the day off. Let's take a moment to look at what you are asking for.

1. There are 365 days available for work.

2. There are 52 weeks per year, of which you already have 2 days off each weekend, leaving 261 days left available for work.

3. Since you spend 16 hours each day away from work, that accounts for 170 days. There are 91 left available for work.

4. You spend 30 minutes each day on breaks, that accounts for 23 days a year, leaving 68 days available for work.

5. You spend 1 hour a day at lunch, accounting for another 46 days per year, leaving 22 days available for work.

6. You spend 2 days per year on sick leave, leaving 20 days available for work.

7. You take 9 holidays per year, leaving 11 days available for work.

8. You take 10 days vacation each year, leaving 1 day left available for work.

No way are you going to take *that* day off.   —Source unknown

Illustrations

A Cheer for Fishing Nets

The *New York Times* reported an incident in an impoverished country. Relief workers distributed food to a long line of citizens who waited quietly in line.

But when they distributed fishing nets, the same people cheered.[104]

Quotes

Salespersons Should Never Be Ashamed

Salespersons should never be ashamed of their calling. They should be ashamed of their *not* calling.   —Albert Lasker[105]

Without Ambition

Without ambition, one starts nothing. Without work, one finishes nothing. The prize will not be sent to you, you have to win it.

—Ralph Waldo Emerson[106]

Martin Luther King Jr.

Illustrations

Martin Luther King's Biography

Born in Atlanta on January 15, 1929, Martin Luther King's roots were in the African-American Baptist church. He was the grandson of the Rev. A. D. Williams, pastor of Ebenezer Baptist church and a founder of Atlanta's NAACP chapter, and the son of Martin Luther King Sr., who succeeded Williams as Ebenezer's pastor and also became a civil rights leader. He greatly admired black social gospel proponents who saw the church as an instrument for improving the lives of African Americans.

Graduating from Morehouse College, he continued theological studies at Crozer Theological Seminary in Chester, Pennsylvania, and at Boston University, where he received a doctorate in systematic theology in 1955. Rejecting offers for academic positions, King decided while completing his Ph.D. requirements to return to the South and accepted the pastorate of Dexter Avenue Baptist Church in Montgomery, Alabama.   —Clayborne Carson[107]

Singing and the Civil Rights Movement

Music dominated the background of the civil rights movement. When the marchers marched, they sang. When they sat patiently waiting for a better day, they sang. At the 1963 march in Washington, it was music that moved the bodies, souls, and minds of the people, as Singer Mahalia Jackson prepared the crowd for the memorable speech by Martin Luther King Jr.

—Emerson B. Powery[108]

Mother's Day

Humor

Baby Comforts Mother

A young mother had a totally exasperating day. The two-year-old had written with a crayon all over the living room wall. The washing machine broke. The VCR quit playing. And the dog chewed through the kitchen wall telephone wire.

Totally frustrated, the mom sat on a chair beside her one-year-old, who was splashing in the bowl of Jell-O on her high-chair tray. Soon the frustrated mom put her arm on the tray, buried her head in her arm, and began to sob.

With a sticky hand and a warm heart, the one-year-old took a pacifier out of her mouth and pushed it into her mother's mouth. And with the other sticky hand, she calmly patted her mother on the head.   —Source unknown

Bedtime Prayers

A mother was hearing her little girl's bedtime prayers. The little girl asked, "Is Grandma still downstairs?"

"Yes she is," her mother replied.

The little girl continued her prayer, but raised the volume to a yell, "AND GOD, YOU KNOW HOW MUCH I WANT A COMPUTER . . ."

Mother interrupted, "You don't have to yell, honey, God's not deaf."

The little girl replied, "I know, but Grandma is."[109]

A Concerned Mother

One wintry morning, a concerned mother called the school principal. She wanted to know if her son's bus had arrived yet. When asked what grade he was in, the mother replied, "Oh, he is not one of the students, he drives the bus!"[110]

I Didn't Do Anything Today

One day, a father came home from work to find his home in total chaos. The children were playing on the lawn in their pajamas. The front door was open. Inside, the furniture was scattered. A shattered lamp lay on the floor. The TV was blaring.

In the kitchen, the sink was full of stacked dishes, cereal was spilled on the floor. Heading upstairs to the bedroom, he passed clothing strung along the banister, stepped over toys on the steps, and climbed over a plant that had spilled onto the floor.

In the bedroom, he was shocked to see his wife still in bed, watching a talk show on the spare TV. She asked how his day went.

He replied, "What in the world has happened here?!"

She answered, "Well, every day, when you arrive home from work, you ask me if I did anything today."

"And?"

"And, today I didn't!"   —Source unknown

Mother's Ten Commandments of Eating

1. Of all the beasts of the field, and of the fish of the sea shalt thou eat. But of the leaves of the tree, thou shalt not eat thereof. For in the day that thou eatest, thou shalt surely get a stomach-ache.

2. Thou shalt drink of all the good liquids I have given unto thee. Only let not thy liquids be spilled onto thy clothing nor onto thy neighbor's clothing.

3. When thou sittest in thy chair, thou shalt not place thy feet on the table nor over thine head. For that is an abomination to me.

4. Thou shalt not pour Kool-Aid over thy mashed potatoes, nor use it as a dip for thy celery, nor spill it over the floor of the place of eating.

5. When thou hast drunk of thy cup, it shall not be held to thy face as a mask, nor used to strike thy brother or thy sister upon their head.

6. Thou shalt not eat thy macaroni with thine hands. Neither shalt thou distribute it widely over the place where thou livest.

7. Thy brussels sprouts shalt not be made into any graven image in the place where thou eatest. That is an abomination to me.

8. When thou sittest in thine chair, thou shalt not slideth down therein.

9. Remember thy mealtime to arrive when I calleth thee. Three meals thou hast been given to cause thy borders to increase.

10. If thou keepest all these commandments I have given unto thee, thou shalt be perfect in my sight, and perfect in my neighbor's sight.   —Jerry Brecheisen

Refrigerator Artwork

A man spent a great sum of money on a brand-new computer. It had the latest in word processing and desktop publishing capabilities.

Wanting to impress his mother, he wrote her a long letter in a beautiful typeface and illustrated it with elaborate clip art. Several days later, he called to see if she received the letter.

"Yes, I received it. Son, you did a fine job. I hung it by your other picture on the refrigerator."[111]

Normal Family

It's getting more difficult to define a "normal family." In one stepparent home, the sister went to her real father's home every other weekend. The brother stayed with his mother and stepfather. As she was leaving the house, he commented, "Must be nice to get a new family every other weekend. I'm stuck here with the same one!"[112]

The Biggest Piece

Sitting around the family table for supper, the youngest child spotted the dessert. With eager hands he reached for the biggest piece of chocolate cake on the plate.

Grabbing his hand with a scolding look, the mother said, "Son, I'm ashamed of you! Why did you take the biggest piece?"

The son replied with chocolate frosting all over his face, "Well, Mom, with this bunch, looks like that's the only way I was gonna get it!"   —Source unknown

The Folded Handkerchief

While talking to his wife, Henry pulled out his handkerchief and blew his nose. After several loud snorts, he folded the white handkerchief into a perfect square and put it in his pocket.

His wife quickly responded, "Henry, do you always fold your handkerchief like that?"

"Of course I do," the husband replied. "'Been folding it like that for fifty years."

Henry's wife spoke up, "Henry, I don't know how to tell you this, but for fifty years, when I've found your handkerchief neatly folded like that in your pocket, I've just assumed that it was clean and put it back in your dresser drawer."

Henry shook his head, "No wonder I've always had such trouble getting my glasses clean."   —Source unknown

The Princess and the Frog

Once upon a time a beautiful princess encountered a frog in a pond.

The frog spoke to the princess: "I used to be a handsome prince until someone put an evil spell on me. If you kiss me on my nose, I will become a prince once again."

"Then we can be married, move into my mother's castle, and you can clean the castle, bear children, cook the meals, and live happily ever after with your handsome prince."

The beautiful princess had frog legs for supper.[113]

When I Fall Down

On a Mother's Day card: "Now that we have a mature, adult relationship, there is something I'd like to tell you. You're still the first person I think of when I fall down and go boom!"

—Derl G. Keefer

Worst-Case Scenario

In the cartoon *Calvin and Hobbes,* Calvin asks his mother, "Can Hobbes and I go play in the rain?"

Mom replies, "Of course not!"

"Why?" Calvin asks.

"You'll get soaked."

Calvin replies, "What's wrong with getting soaked?"

Mom answers, "You could catch cold, run up a big doctor bill, linger for a few months, and then die."

Calvin looks forlornly out the window. "I forgot. If you ask a mom, you always get a worst-case scenario."[114]

Your Wife and I Haven't Been Getting Along

Father came home from work and found his young daughter sitting under a tree by the driveway. Noticing her sad countenance, he inquired, "What's wrong, dear?"

She replied, "Well, Dad, your wife and I haven't been getting along that great today." —William Turner[115]

Illustrations

Erin's Pride

When I was 13, I built a pigeon coop and raced pigeons with the local Racing Pigeon Association. Pigeon owners don't let the birds eat wet corn, since the grain will swell up in their gullets and choke them.

One night some grain that I had left for the pigeons became wet. My prize pigeon ate it and her gullet swelled.

"She's gonna die," I yelled, and ran into the house to tell Mother. After several procedures failed, she announced "We'll operate."

"She'll die," I said.

"She'll die anyway," Mother replied.

The dining room table became the operating table. Mother sterilized the "equipment," plucked the feathers from the pigeon's neck, and washed it with alcohol.

With a single incision, she sliced the bird's neck from the head to breast. The bird flayed, but I held the wings steady. Mother thrust her fingers into the neck and retrieved the corn. Then, using a sterilized needle and sewing thread, she stitched the bird's neck back together. "Just like darning a sock," she said.

The pigeon lived and I called her "Erin's Pride," after my Mother. Later, Erin's Pride won the 500-mile race from Gulf Port, Mississippi, to Savannah, Georgia.

"We're Townses," she had previously announced, "we can do anything we want to do." —Elmer Towns

Grant's Mother

When Civil War General Ulysses S. Grant's mother died, he said to the minister who was to officiate at the funeral: "Make no reference to me. She owed nothing to me. Speak of her just as she was, a pure-minded, simple-hearted, earnest Christian."

—Clarence Macartney[116]

Mama Told Me Not To

I always remember a comment by Judge Elbert Tuttle, one of the great jurists of our country. A republican appointed by President Eisenhower, he made some of the most definitive and courageous rulings on civil rights during the troubled segregation days in Georgia. Walter Cronkite once interviewed him, "Judge Tutle, I understand you've never drunk whiskey."

The judge said, "I've never in my life tasted an alcoholic drink."

Cronkite asked, "Why not?"

The judge gave a simple reply, "Because my mama told me not to."

—Jimmy Carter[117]

The Grandmother of Us All

Henrietta Mears has been called the "mother of Sunday School." But I like to think of her more as the "grandmother" of modern evangelicalism. She used to say, "There is no magic in small plans. When I consider my ministry, I think of the world. Anything less than that would not be worthy of Christ nor of his will for my life." So while inspiring her "college boys" with her hats, she also imparted to them the vision of conquering the world for Christ. And her "boys" included the likes of Campus Crusade's Bill Bright and former U.S. Senate chaplain, the late Richard Halverson.

—Wendy Murray Zoba[118]

Quotes

Children Brighten the Home

Children brighten the home. Which one of them ever turns off a light?

—*Christian Herald*

Mother's Concern

Franklin Roosevelt reported that even after he became President of the United States, he never went outdoors without his mother calling after him, "Franklin! Are you sure you're dressed warmly enough?"[119]

Mother Made Me Believe

Mother made me believe that the average person can rise above circumstances even with limited resources and in difficult circumstances, and get the job done.   —Elmer Towns

Motherhood Is Full of Frustrations

Motherhood is full of frustrations and challenges—but eventually they move out.[120]

Extension of Their Dreams

Mothers exercise the greatest influences on our self-perception because we are the extension of their dreams, values, and prejudices. A mother usually expects her children to become more than she became and accomplish more than she achieved.

—Elmer Towns

Mothers Fill Places

Mothers fill places so great that there isn't an angel in heaven who wouldn't be glad to give a bushel of diamonds to come down here and take their place.   —Billy Sunday[121]

My Sunset Prayer

As once she stroked my tiny head
With a softness like the sand,
I touch her thin and silv'ry strands
And hold her trembling hand;
As once she viewed my learning feet
With a firm but anxious care,
I watch her failing, bending gait
And breathe my sunset prayer,
"O Lord, since I'm her precious child
From some great other time,
Help me to love her even more,
Since the years have made her mine."

—Adapted by Jerry Brecheisen

The Day

The day the child realizes that all adults are imperfect, he becomes an adolescent. The day he forgives them, he becomes an adult. The day he forgives himself, he becomes wise.[122]

Only One Child

There's only one child in the world, and every mother has it.

—English Proverb

With Great Love

We can do no great things—only small things with great love.

—Mother Teresa[123]

My Mother

Who ran to help me when I fell,
And would some pretty story tell,
Or kiss the wound to make it well?
My mother.

—Jane Taylor, "My Mother"

National Day of Prayer

Humor

Say What Mom Says

On a steaming hot day, family guests were seated around the table. Mother asked her four-year-old to say grace.

"I don't know what to say!" the little boy responded.

"Just say what you've heard your mom say," the mother replied.

The little boy bowed reverently, "Lord! Why did I invite these folks on a day like this!"   —Mark Hollingsworth

Illustrations

How Jesus Prayed

1. He prayed early (Mark 1:35-37).

2. He prayed late (Matt. 14:23).
3. He prayed all night (Luke 6:12).
4. He prayed before events (Luke 6:12-13).
5. He prayed for His friends (Luke 22:31).
6. He prayed until the heavens opened (Luke 3:21).
7. He prayed as He died (Luke 23:46).

—Stan Toler

The Obituary of Mrs. Prayer Meeting

Mrs. Prayer Meeting died recently at the First Neglected Church, on Busy Ave. Born many years ago in the midst of great revivals, she was a strong, healthy child, fed largely on prayers, testimony, and Bible study. She had become one of the most influential members of the famous Church family.

For the past several years, Mrs. Prayer Meeting has been failing in health, suffering stiffness of knees, coldness of heart, inactivity, and weakness of purpose and willpower.

Doctors of Religious Works had administered large doses of organization, recreation, contests, and drives, but to no avail. An autopsy showed that a deficiency of faith, heartfelt religion, and general support contributed to her death.

Survivors include several sobbing saints who mourned her past glory.   —Stan Toler

Quotes

The Greater Work

Prayer does not equip us for greater works—prayer is the greater work.   —Oswald Chambers

New Year

Humor

Things I Ought to Do

A teen sat at the kitchen table on New Year's Eve, writing on a tablet. His mother entered the room, "What are you doing?"

He replied, "I'm writing a list of things I ought to do in the New Year. I'm calling it my OUGHTTOBIOGRAPHY."[124]

The Resolution I Can Keep

In the cartoon *For Better or Worse* the family is sitting around the dinner table on New Year's Day making their resolutions.

Mother starts, "I resolve to criticize less and bake more." The family shouts their approval.

Elizabeth adds, "I resolve to take care of the dog, keep my room clean, and not fight with my brother."

Father resolves, "I will not lose my temper and I'll fix everything in the house that needs fixing." Mother nods in approval.

Michael announces, "I resolve to ride my bike, hang out with my friends, and watch a lot of TV."

Mother replies, "What kind of a resolution is that?"

Michael says, "The kind I can keep!"[125]

Illustrations

A Philosophy of Life

An elderly man was asked his philosophy of life. He replied:
- "Don't work any harder any day than you can recover by sleep at night.
- Eat simple foods.
- Exercise and sleep, and take plenty of time for recreation.
- With the time that is left, make as much money as you can and be content with it.
- Don't overdraw your nervous capital.
- Don't overcrowd time."[126]

Follow the Banner

Asked the secret of her victories, Joan of Arc was said to have answered, "I send my banner forward against the enemy, and then I follow it myself."[127]

Live Today

Written on the margins of the Bible John Wesley preached from: "Live today."[128]

Looking Forward and Backward

January is the month of beginnings. *Janua* in Latin means a door. From that came the name of Janus, Ancient Roman god of all beginnings. Janus had two faces so that he might look both forward and back at the same time. He presided over gateways, bridges, doors, and entrances. In his honor, the first month of the year was called January by Pompilius in the seventh century before Christ.[129]

New Growth

Asked later in life how he managed to age so well, the poet Longfellow pointed to an apple tree, "That apple tree is very old, but I never saw prettier blossoms on it. It grows a little every year, and I suppose that it is out of that new growth that the blossoms come. Like that apple tree, I try to grow a little every year."

—Source unknown

Put Something Beautiful into Every Day

A college student hung a new wall calendar in her dorm room and declared, "It's going to be a great New Year."

Her roommate asked, "How do you know that? A lot of things could happen this year. A year is a very long time."

She replied, "It will be a beautiful year because I am going to live it one day at a time. And I am going to make sure I put something beautiful into every one of those days."

—Source unknown

Try Again

The New Year is a chance to try again.

A famous painter was asked which of his pictures he considered his best. He replied, "The next."   —Source unknown

Quotes

A.D.

The world writes the letters carelessly as it turns the page to record for the first time the new year; but in these letters is the "open secret" of the ages, this, too, is a "year of our Lord," and "an acceptable year," a "year of grace."   —Jesse B. Thomas

Auld Lang Syne

> *Should auld acquaintance be forgot,*
> *And never brought to mind?*
> *Should auld acquaintance be forgot,*
> *And auld lang syne!*

> —Robert Burns

A Better Man

Be at war with your vices, at peace with your neighbors, and let every new year find you a better man.   —Benjamin Franklin

God Bless Your Year

> *God bless your year!*
> *Your coming in, your going out,*
> *Your rest, your traveling about,*
> *The tough, the smooth,*
> *The bright, the drear,*
> *God bless your year!*

> —Source unknown

Good Resolutions Are like Babies

Good resolutions are like babies crying in church. They should be carried out immediately.   —Charles M. Sheldon[130]

I Asked the New Year

> *I asked the New Year for some message sweet,*
> *Some rule of life with which to guide my feet;*
> *I asked, and paused: he answered soft and low,*
> *"God's will to know!"*

"Will knowledge then suffice, New Year?" I cried;
And ere the question into silence died,
The answer came, "Remember, too,
God's will to do!"

Once more I asked, "Is there no more to tell?"
And once again the answer sweetly fell,
"Yes! This thing, all other things above:
God's will to love!"[131]

At the Gate of the New Year

I said to the man who stands at the Gate of the Year, "Give me light that I may tread softly into the unknown!" And he replied, "Step into the darkness, put your hand into the hand of God, and that will be to you better than a light and safer than a known way!"

—King George VI

Mistakes

- Mistakes are friends that help me see myself.
- Mistakes are keys that unlock the door of opportunity.
- Mistakes are windows that help me look at the world.
- Mistakes are prophecies that help me understand the future.
- Mistakes are teachers that give me insight into life.
- Mistakes are poetry that help me see how things fit together.
- Mistakes are the paint I use for the portrait of life.

—Elmer Towns

The Gift of Time

Time is a wonderful thing. All men have it, and all have precisely the same amount of it. The gift is given you a little at a time. You must use it at once or it is withdrawn.　　—Amos R. Wells

The Second Best Time

A sign in front of a greenhouse read: "The best time to plant a tree was 25 years ago. The second best time is today."　　—Stan Toler

Win the Future

You can never change the past. But by the grace of God, you can win the future. So remember those things which will help you forward, but forget those things which will only hold you back.

—Richard C. Woodsome[132]

Pentecost Sunday

Quotes

Age of the Spirit

We do not need another Pentecost . . . we live in the age of the Spirit.   —William Greathouse

Deposit on Future Inheritance

The Holy Spirit was given to believers at Pentecost as a deposit on our future inheritance in Christ.   —Thomas Hermiz

Rise to the Stature of God

If the church is to rise to its fullest stature in God, if it is to enjoy the abundant life, if it is to meet all foes in the spirit of triumph, it must rely not upon its numbers or skills, but upon the power of the Holy Spirit.   —Arthur Moore

Center of Holiness

Pentecost is the center of holiness. Experience the glory of the Spirit's presence among us.   —Derl Keefer

Sanctity of Life

Illustrations

When Life Begins

Too much is now known of human development to seriously debate when life begins.

At 18 to 25 days, the heart is beating.

At 40 days, brain waves can be recorded.

At 11 to 12 weeks, the baby can suck his or her thumb and is sensitive to heat, touch, and light. —Stephen Nelson[133]

Quotes

Two Victims in Abortion

There are two victims in abortion—the child who dies and the mother who bears the emotional and psychological scars.

—Stephen Nelson[134]

Stewardship

Humor

Does God Do Windows?

During his message on stewardship, a preacher announced that God promised He would open the windows of heaven for those who tithe.

Later, he was asked about the percentage, "What about 5 percent?"

"No!" the preacher replied, "God doesn't do windows for less than 10 percent!" —Stan Toler

Give 'Til It Hurts

The chairman of the building fund announced the fall stewardship campaign theme. "Our theme is 'Giving Until It Hurts,'" he said enthusiastically.

When he heard the announcement, one of the church members, a man who was not known for his generosity, turned to his wife and whispered, "Frankly, Bertha, the whole thing gives me a pain!"[135]

Stop Printing Dollar Bills

The church treasurer was lamenting the small amount in the Sunday offering. Talking with the pastor later in the week, he told him he came up with an idea that would add new financial growth to the church.

"Pastor, let's petition the government to stop printing one-dollar bills!"   —Stan Toler

I'm Thinking

One of the most celebrated tightwads in history, Jack Benny, tells of being approached by a mugger while he was walking down a street.

"Your money or your life," the mugger demanded.

There was a long pause.

"Well?" the robber prodded.

Benny replied, "Don't rush me. I'm thinking! I'm thinking!"

—Source unknown

Give It to the Church

A woman called a food distributor with a question about preparing her Thanksgiving Day turkey.

"The turkey has been in the freezer for 10 years, is it safe to eat?"

The operator advised, "It will be all right if the freezer thermostat has been kept near zero degrees." She continued, "However, I'll have to warn you that there is probably a loss of flavor."

"Just what I thought!" the woman replied, "I'll just give it to the church."   —Stan Toler

Pay Where You Sleep

A man built a house across the Arkansas-Missouri line. County officials were confused on how to charge taxes. But the tax law stated that a man must pay taxes according to where he sleeps.

Officials from the state of Arkansas arrived unexpectedly one night in hopes of finding a discrepancy. To their dismay, they looked into the window and saw that the man had positioned his bed directly over the state line.   —C. Gordan Bayless[136]

Squeezing an Orange Dry

The strong man at the circus concluded his show with a simple but impressive demonstration of his ability to squeeze an orange dry. At the end of his act, he would challenge anyone from the audience to come forward and try to extract even one drop from the crushed orange.

On one occasion, a little man, built like Barney Fife, volunteered. Everyone snickered. Undaunted, the little guy stepped onto the stage and took the shriveled-up piece of fruit from the strong man. A hush came over the circus tent as the audience watched in amazement this small-framed man squeeze out a glass full of orange juice.

After the cheers subsided, the strong man asked the little guy how he did it. Modestly, the little fellow said, "Nothin' to it. I'm the treasurer at the Baptist Church."   —Stan Toler

The Talking Parrot

Advised to buy a pet for some companionship, a lonely widow went to a pet store. The store clerk gave her several options but the widow settled on a beautiful parrot. "Does it talk?" the widow asked.

The clerk replied, "Talk? You won't be able to shut it up!"

The widow paid for the bird and took it home with great anticipation.

Two weeks later, the widow called the pet store. "Remember that talking parrot you sold me?"

"Of course," the clerk answered.

"Hasn't said one word!" the widow said in disgust.

The widow was told to come to the store and the clerk sold her some bird supplies. The widow quickly put them in the cage, hoping for a few words from her parrot companion.

First, she installed a little mirror so the parrot would see its reflection and comment. Not a word.

Second, she put a replica of a tree branch in the cage so the parrot could exercise. Not a word.

Third, she put a bell in the cage so the bird could display its musical talents. Not a word.

Calling the pet store again, she said sadly. "My beautiful parrot is dead."

"Dead?" the store clerk exclaimed. "Did it say anything?"

"Yes, finally. As it lay on the bottom of the cage with its feet in the air, it said, "Did you ever think of buying some bird feed for this cage?""
                                                                  —Stan Toler

Three Offerings

A miserly but devout parishioner listened to the announcement of the offering. "There will be three offerings: one for the regular offering, one for the building fund, and another for missions."

He had forgotten to change the batteries in his hearing aid and so he really didn't understand what the pastor was announcing.

He gave in the first offering.

Astonished, he gave in the second offering.

As the usher handed him the plate for the third offering, he pulled the usher down to him by his tie, "What are you going to do now, frisk me?"
                                                      —Mark Hollingsworth

Walking Economy

"I'm a walking economy," a man was overheard to say. "My hairline's in recession, my waist is a victim of inflation, and together they are putting me into a deep depression."   —Milton Segal[137]

Illustrations

12 Tools for Cultivating an Unselfish Church

1. Plan ahead.
2. Emphasize discipleship.
3. Bathe in prayer.
4. Identify specific goals.
5. Get commitments.
6. Involve more people.
7. Build trust.
8. Build relationships.
9. Model generosity.
10. Be positive.
11. Spell out sacrifice.
12. Point out the reward.
                                                      —Jay Pankratz[138]

A Stewardship Puzzle

Write down the year of your birth.

Double it—multiply by 50.

Add your age—the first four numbers of the answer will be the year you were born and the last two your age.

NOW—write down your salary.

Subtract 90 percent.

The balance is the Lord's.

Give it to Him, and watch how He will bless the 90 percent.

—Source unknown

The Beauty of Giving

During the American Revolution there lived a Baptist pastor by the name of Peter Miller. He was a man who enjoyed the friendship of George Washington. In the same city lived another man, named Michael Whitman, an ungodly scoundrel who did everything in his power to obstruct and oppose the work of the pastor.

Whitman was involved in an act of treason against the United States. He was arrested and taken to Philadelphia, 70 miles away, to appear before Washington. When the news reached Miller, he walked the 70 miles to Philadelphia to appeal for the life of his enemy.

Admitted to the presence of General Washington, he began to speak for Whitman's life. Washington heard his story through, then said, "No, Peter, I cannot give you the life of your friend." Peter Miller said, "My friend! This man is not my friend. He is the bitterest enemy I have."

Washington said, "You have walked 70 miles through the dust and the heat of the road to appeal for the life of your enemy? Well, that puts this matter in a different light. I will give you, then, the life of your enemy." Miller put his arm around the shoulders of Michael Whitman and led him out of the very shadow of death back to his own home, no longer his enemy but a friend.

When we were enemies, when we were yet without strength, helpless, opposed to God, rebelling again His precepts and principles, leading self-centered lives without regard for His rights, using His goods and His resources, Christ Jesus died for us. That is the beauty of stewardship. That is the beauty of giving.

—Elmer Towns[139]

The Giving Lesson

A group of students from a Christian college journeyed to Mexico. Once there, they ministered to families living in cardboard huts near a dump.

Three boys, dirty and shabbily dressed, played near the dump. Through an interpreter, a college student gave one of the boys a single piece of gum.

In a lesson in giving, the boy took the piece of gum, nodded to the student, and tore the gum into three pieces—a piece for each of his friends.[140]

The Savior Is Watching the Offering

To the amazement of his congregation, a well-known pastor accompanied his ushers as they walked the aisles receiving the offering one Sunday.

He later announced from the pulpit, "I have seen your offerings and know what sacrifices you have made or not made. I did this as a reminder that the Savior walks the aisles every Sunday and He sees every cent put into the collection by His people."

—William Ward[141]

Treasure in the Backyard

The troubles of a young couple escalated. The husband was laid off from his job and then the plumbing in their house went bad.

Digging in the backyard for the water line, they were astonished to uncover a gold coin. That prompted further excavation. Before it was done, their trouble had turned to treasure. They had apparently stumbled on the bounty of some Gold Rush era prospectors and now owned a coin collection of over $1 million.

—*Illusaurus*[142]

Quotes

Each Time We Write a Check

Each time we write a check it would be wise to remember we are but bankers who manage the Lord's account.   —Ron Blue

Effective Resource Development

Effective resource development is not a money grab. It has a spiritual foundation that makes discipleship its primary goal. The key to resource development is growth in people.   —Jay Pankratz[143]

Make a Life

From what we get, we make a living; what we give, however, makes a life.   —Arthur Ashe

God Demands Our Tithes

God demands our tithes and deserves our offerings.
                                            —Stephen Olford[144]

God Gives to Us

God gives *to us* what He knows will flow *through us.*
                                            —Robert Schuller[145]

Channels for Sharing

God has given us two hands—one to receive with and the other to give with. We are not cisterns made for hoarding; we are channels made for sharing.   —Billy Graham[146]

Wesley's Advice

Make all you can, save all you can, give all you can.
                                            —John Wesley

The Ultimate Resource

Many of us live more for the world that is going than the world that is coming. It takes time, lots of time, to manage all the "things" we accumulate. Time, in the final analysis, is the ultimate resource.
                                            —Patrick Morley[147]

Tithing an Outward Expression

Tithing is simply an outward expression of spiritual growth, and spiritual growth leads to material growth.
                                            —Sir John Templeton[148]

Lifestyle from a Checkbook

You can't fake stewardship. Your checkbook reveals all that you really believe about stewardship. A lifestyle could be written from a checkbook.   —Ron Blue[149]

Super Bowl

Humor

Football and Church Definitions

- Draft choice: Selection of a seat near the door.
- Halftime: The time between the prayer and the offertory.
- Benchwarmer: Those whose only participation is their attendance on Sunday morning.
- Quarterback sneak: Parishioners who exit quietly following Communion, a quarter of the way through the service or near the last quarter of service.
- Fumble: Dropping a worship folder.
- Backfield in motion: Making two or three trips out during the sermon.
- Staying in the pocket: What happens to a lot of money that should go to missions.
- Sudden death: When the preacher goes overtime.
- Blitz: The stampede to the doors after the service.[150]

Thanksgiving

Humor

A Politically Correct Thanksgiving

The politically correct fourth grader reported on the origins of Thanksgiving to his class: "The pilgrims came here seeking freedom of . . . you know what. When they landed, they gave thanks to . . . you know who. Because of them, we can worship . . . you know where."   —Stan Toler

God Is Great

An elderly man sat on a folding chair on the porch of a local nursing home with his Bible in his lap. Suddenly he shouted, "God is great!"

A ministry intern came over to him and sat in the next chair. "Can't help but hear you talk about God."

"I just read how He parted the waters of the Red Sea and led the Israelites right through," the man said.

"That's right," the intern responded, "I just studied that in Bible school. But did you know that scholars tell us the Red Sea was only about ten inches deep at the time?"

"Well, that makes Him greater than I thought!" the older man shouted.

"What do you mean?" the smarmy intern asked.

The elderly man replied, "He not only led those Israelite folk through the Red Sea, He drowned the enemy in less than a foot of water."   —Mark Hollingsworth

I Just Can't Find the Words

A college student received a call from her mother. "Honey, I sent you a new collegiate dictionary in the mail. Did you get it?"

"Oh, Mother," the student replied. "That was so thoughtful of you! I just can't find the words to thank you."[151]

Thanksgiving Memories

Two turkeys were reminiscing about their Thanksgiving holidays. One remarked, "Tell me about your holiday?"

The second turkey answered, "I celebrated it the day after Thanksgiving!"   —Stan Toler

Illustrations

Gratitude in Tragedy

A missionary visited the home of one of her national worker colleagues at the news of her brother's death. Entering a tiny room, where the worker and over a dozen other relatives lived, she went to speak to the mother.

Expressing her condolences to the lady who was sitting on a grass mat, she was surprised that the mother suddenly began to express her gratitude. Pointing around the tiny room, the lady began, "Thank you for hiring my daughter. Because of you, we have paint on the wall. You helped to fix the roof that leaked. If you hadn't hired my daughter, we wouldn't have been able to buy screens to keep the mosquitoes out."

The list went on. And the missionary left, humbled by the profound gratitude expressed in a tragic situation.   —Faith Finley[152]

How Much?

A man traveled the country of France but knew only one word in the French language: *"Combien?"* It means, "How much?" There are many that have just one standard of values. They speak only the language of money, "How much?"   —J. Wallace Hamilton[153]

Thanksgiving in Any Language

"Dad! Guess what?" a junior high student announced. "I can say 'Thanks' in Spanish!"

"That's great!" the father commented. "When are you going to learn it in English?"   —Stan Toler

Quotes

Thankfulness

It is always possible to be thankful for what is given rather than to complain about what is not given. One or the other becomes a habit of life.   —Elisabeth Elliott

Symphony with No Applause

No action can be truly complete without gratitude. A symphony without applause at the end isn't a completed symphony.
                    —Peter Stewart[154]

The Unthankful Heart

The unthankful heart, like my finger in the sand, discovers no mercies; but let the thankful heart sweep through the day, and as the magnet finds the iron, so it will find, in every hour, some heavenly blessings; only the iron in God's sand is gold!

—Henry Ward Beecher

A Helping Hand

There is no lovelier way to thank God for your sight than by giving a helping hand to someone in the dark.   —Helen Keller[155]

Valentine's Day

Humor

I Wish to Understand Women

A man walking along the beach in Hawaii finds a lamp. He rubs it and a genie pops out. Thankful for his release, the genie tells the man he will grant him two wishes.

"Let's see," the man rubs his chin and thinks out loud. "I'd like a highway back to California because I'm afraid to fly."

Immediately the genie responds, "I'm afraid that is technically impossible, considering the ocean depth and the distance from here to California. Try something else and I promise I will grant you your wish."

"Well then, Mr. Genie, my second wish is to be able to understand women."

The genie slowly shakes his head and replies, "Would you like two lanes or four lanes on that highway?"   —Sharon Boso[156]

The 50/50 Marriage

A young man saw an elderly couple sitting down to lunch at McDonald's. He noticed that they had ordered one meal and an extra cup. As he watched, the gentleman carefully divided the hamburger in half, then counted out fries, one for her, one for him, until each had half of them. Then he poured half of the soft drink into the extra cup and set it in front of his wife.

The elderly gentleman then began to eat, his wife watched with her hands folded in her lap. The young man decided to ask them if they wouldn't mind it if he purchased another meal so they wouldn't have to share. The old man said, "Oh, no. We've been married 50 years and we split everything 50/50."

The young man then asked the wife if she was going to eat her share of the meal and she replied, "Not yet. It's his turn to use the teeth."   —Stan Toler

The Order of the Mustard Seed

The *Order of the Mustard Seed,* founded by Count Zinzendorf, had three guiding principles: (1) Be kind to all, (2) Seek to be good to all, (3) Win them all to Christ.[157]

Top 10 Reasons Why I Know I'm an Improving Husband

10. I put my dishes in the sink so she can easily put them into the dishwasher.
 9. I let my wife drive the better car even if it isn't low on gas.
 8. I almost never tell the children, "Go ask your mother."
 7. I can watch TV and pretend I'm listening to a conversation at the same time.
 6. I can change a vacuum cleaner belt and bag without a nervous breakdown.
 5. I can fold laundry without written instructions.
 4. I seek my wife's guidance in important matters such as finding my car keys.
 3. I almost never ask my wife to carry my golf clubs.
 2. I know how to spell *romanse.*
 1. I have learned how to salute and say, "Yes, Ma'am!"
                                                       —Jeffrey Johnson

Illustrations

Better than Salt

A monarch called his three daughters to him. "How much do you love your Father?" he asked.

Two of the daughter replied that they loved him more than gold and silver.

"And how about you?" the king said to the third daughter.

She replied, "Father, I love you more than salt."

The answer didn't please the king. "Salt?" he thought. "What a strange remark!"

The cook of the royal household overheard the [daughter's] remark. . . . The next morning, the king's breakfast was prepared without any seasoning. It was bland and tasteless. The king summoned the cook, "Why is my breakfast so tasteless?"

"There is no salt on it, your majesty," the cook replied.

His daughter's words came to mind. The king understood. His daughter loved him so much that nothing was good without him.

—A. C. Dixon

Children's Philosophy of Love

- "One of the people has freckles and so he finds somebody else who has freckles too." Andrew, age 6.

- "No one is sure why it happens, but I heard it has something to do with how you smell. That's why perfume and deodorant are so popular." Mae, age 9.

- "I think you're supposed to get shot with an arrow or something, but the rest of it isn't supposed to be so painful." Manuel, age 8.

- "Love is like an avalanche where you have to run for your life." John, age 9.

- "If falling in love is anything like learning how to spell, I don't want to do it. It takes too long." Glenn, age 7.

—Source unknown

A Circle Goes on Forever

In the cartoon Family Circus, Billy and Dolly are drawing valentines. Dolly draws the traditional valentine heart but Billy opts for a valentine circle. His explanation, "Instead of a heart I drew a circle. A heart can be broken but a circle goes on forever."

—Bill Keane[158]

Wedding

Quotes

Most Brilliant Achievement

My most brilliant achievement was my ability to persuade my wife
to marry me.   —Winston Churchill

Two Such as You

Two such as you with
such a master speed
Cannot be parted
nor be swept away
From one another
once you are agreed
That life is only
Life forevermore
Together
Wing to wing
And oar to oar.

—Robert Frost

📁 *File Folder*

Be Yourself

We're all human. We're all a little afraid of the podium, the microphone, or the boardroom. Despite what you may believe, people
don't want you to fail. They ultimately want to see you succeed.
Give them what they want by just being the best you can be.[159]

📁 *File Folder*

Practice

Practice and rehearse your speech at home or where you can be
at ease and comfortable, in front of a mirror, your family, friends,
or colleagues. Use a tape recorder and listen to yourself. Video-
tape your presentation and analyze it. Know what your strong and
weak points are. Emphasize your strong points during your presentation.[160]

9
SPEAKER HELPS

Openers

Humor

A Special Prayer Request

A little boy was having trouble behaving in church.

Finally, the exasperated father picked him up, threw him over his shoulder, and marched down the center aisle.

Knowing what would happen when they reached the foyer, the little boy raised his hand and shouted to the audience, "Folks, I have a special prayer request!"

—Executive Speechwriters Newsletter

Bad Luck

An elderly man and his wife of more than 60 years were sitting on a swing in the backyard, reminiscing.

Fred said, "Martha, for 60 years you've been at my side. You were there when I was drafted and had to go off to fight in the Korean War. You were there with me when our first house burned to the ground. And you were there when I had the accident that destroyed our little Volkswagen. Yes, you were there when our little shoe shop went belly up and I lost every cent I had."

"Yes, honey," his wife said, patting his hand.

Fred sighed deeply "You know, Martha," he said, "I'm beginning to think you're bad luck!"   —Stan Toler

Baseball in Heaven

Two baseball fanatics agreed that whoever died first would try to come back and tell the other if there was baseball in heaven.

A few months later, one died during the seventh inning stretch at a major league baseball game.

A year later, the remaining fan heard voices in his sleep, "Joe!" "Joe!"

Joe was startled and awoke, "Fred, is that you?"

"Yes," his buddy responded. "I've got some good news and some bad news."

"No kidding! Give me the good news first," he replied.

"Well, the good news is that there *is* baseball up here."

Joe asked, "And the bad?"

"You're scheduled to pitch tomorrow afternoon."

—Source unknown

Death Doesn't Have a Good Track Record

In the cartoon *SHOE,* Skyler holds up his report card and says, "I study all night and get a lousy C. And dumb Lenny lucks out an A!"

His father replies, "You may as well get used to it, Skyler, life isn't fair. But then, death doesn't have a good track record either."

—Source unknown

He Was a Saint

Two brothers were stalwarts in attendance at a local church but were hypocrites who lived a wicked life on the wealth they inherited from their grandfather.

A new pastor was called to their church. It didn't take long for him to learn about the brothers' hypocritical lifestyle. Soon, one of the brothers died, and the preacher was asked to conduct the funeral.

Just before the funeral, the surviving brother pulled the pastor aside and told him he didn't want anything bad said about his brother during the service.

"In fact," the brother advised, "if you tell these folk that my brother was a saint, I'll write you out a check big enough to pay off the mortgage on the church."

The pastor wrestled with the assignment but a few minutes later, he made his way to the front of the funeral chapel and started the service.

"We are gathered here today in loving memory of one of the most wicked men in this community, but next to his brother here, I'm sure we can all agree our departed friend was *a saint!*"

—Source unknown

It Sounds like a Squirrel to Me

The pastor gathered children from the audience for his children's sermon. "Today, boys and girls, we're going to talk about a creature that lives in the forest."

The children listened intently.

The pastor continued, "Sometimes he lives way up in the air and sometimes he crawls around in the backyard, gathering nuts and carrying them to his treehouse."

"Does anyone here know who I'm talking about?"

A little girl sitting near the pastor grabbed his microphone and announced, "The answer's prob'ly 'Jesus,' but it sure does sound like a squirrel to me!"

—Stan Toler

The Last Words

Three brothers were talking about their philosophy of life, and what impact they would have after they went to the Great Beyond. The first brother suddenly asked, "What would you like people to say about you as they stand before your casket?"

The second brother said, "That's easy, I'd like them to say that I was one of the most handsome and articulate persons they had ever met."

The brothers then looked to the third, who responded with a shrug of his shoulder, "I don't know, I guess I'd like someone to say, 'Look! I think I saw him move!'"

—Stan Toler

The Accountability Group

A group of pastors formed an accountability group. At their first meeting in a local restaurant, they began to share their faults.

The first pastor said, "Brothers, I have to confess I'm addicted to late-night TV."

The second pastor responded, "Bless you, brother, I have a need too. I've skipped two church board meetings by calling and saying I was sick when I really wasn't."

The third pastor said nothing.

After a long pause, the other pastors asked compassionately, "Anything you'd like us to pray about, Brother?"

The third pastor nodded, "Yes, I'm afraid so. I have a problem with keeping things in confidence."   —Source unknown

The Brother and Sister Commandment

The Sunday School teacher was reviewing the lessons on the Ten Commandments with his third grade class. "What's the commandment that refers to fathers and mothers?"

"Honor thy father and thy mother," a boy on the front row answered.

"Can you think of another commandment that is important to the family? How about a commandment for brothers and sisters?" he asked.

"*I know,*" a little girl yelled from the back row, "thou shalt not kill!"   —Mark Hollingsworth

Heaven Quiz

A pastor gathered the children around him on the platform for story time. Talking about being good and going to heaven, he asked, "Where do you boys and girls want to go?"

The children shouted the answer, "To heaven!"

"And what do you have to be to go to heaven?" he asked.

A kindergarten boy's face lit up, "I know," he said with assurance.

"OK," the pastor replied, "tell the audience."

The little boy turned around to the audience and gave a one-answer response: "Dead."   —Stan Toler

The Parking Miracle

There's a chain of doughnut stores in Oklahoma called Daylight Donuts. Best in the west! In fact, it's hard to find a parking place in the mornings at Daylight Donuts. One Monday morning, I found myself in spiritual warfare. "Do I stay true to my diet, or do I go to Daylight Donuts for a blueberry, cream-cheese filled doughnut and a diet Coke?" I began to pray, "Lord, You know how busy Daylight Donuts is this time of day. If You want me to have a doughnut, you just make a parking spot available right in front of the store." Don't you know, the seventh time around the block, a miracle parking spot opened up right in front of the door! I believe in miracles!

—Stan Toler

The Speed Limit

A police officer pulled over a carload of women on their way back from a convention. The officer walked up to the car and politely said, "Ma'am, this is a 65-mph highway—why are you going so slowly?"

The driver quickly responded, "Sir, I saw a sign that said 22, not 65!"

The policeman laughingly said, "Oh, that's not the speed limit, that's the name of the highway you're on!"

To which the lady said, "Oh! Silly me! Thanks for letting me know. I'll be more careful."

The policeman then looked in the back seat and saw two other women shaking and trembling. Tenderly the policeman said to the lady, "Excuse me, but what's wrong with your friends back there? They're shaking something terrible."

"Oh, we just got off Highway 121," the lady responded.

—Stan Toler

They're Looking for Me

A little boy answered the phone. "Hello."

A voice on the other end asked for his mother.

The boy replied, "She can't come to the phone. She's outside talking to the policeman."

The caller said, "OK, then let me speak to your dad."

The boy replied, "Sorry. He's outside talking to the policeman."

Curious, the caller asked, "Why is everybody outside talking to the policeman?"

The boy responded in a hushed voice, "They're all looking for me."

—Stan Toler

Try Doing What I Do

A man afraid of thunderstorms went to a well-known psychiatrist. The psychiatrist began to scold him, "Afraid of thunderstorms . . . at your age?"

"I can't help it, Doc," the man replied. "What do you recommend I do?"

"Try doing what I do," the doctor answered.

"What's that?" the patient asked.

"Put cotton in your ears, grab your teddy bear, crawl behind the couch, and sing 'Twinkle, Twinkle, Little Star' as loud as you can."

—Source unknown

Who Signed Me Up?

A six-year-old boy was more than a little bit anxious on his first day of first grade. When the bell finally sounded at noon, he couldn't have been more pleased. He followed all his classmates out the door, down the hall, and into the playground . . . then he kept right on walking toward the gate to freedom.

"Brian," the teacher said when she finally caught up to the student, "why are you leaving school so early?"

"I heard the bell, so I'm going home," he answered assuredly.

"But, Brian," she replied, "you're in the first grade now. School doesn't get out until three o'clock."

Lowering his head, embarrassed and confused, he looked back up at Miss Stewart and said, "What I want to know is, who signed me up for the whole day?"   —Stan Toler

You Missed Your Calling

The pastor had a problem. The worship leader had announced his resignation out of frustration over a certain choir member. The choir member, wife of the chairman of the church board, had been the subject of controversy for several years. She couldn't carry a tune!

The pastor called the tone-deaf choir member to his office. For the next 30 minutes, he tried to tactfully ask the lady to drop out of the choir.

"Why should I quit choir?" she asked.

"Well, Sister, I've had over a dozen people tell me that singing in the choir just isn't your calling."

"That's nothing!" the errant alto replied, "I've had two dozen tell me you missed your calling!"   —Tracy Sims[1]

Illustrations

All the Keys

Lacking power in ministry, the great preacher F. B. Meyer asked a missionary, "Why is God using you and not me?"

The missionary replied, "You must give yourself totally to Jesus."

Later in prayer, Meyer envisioned a ring of keys—the ring of his will and the keys of his life. One key was harder to give, so he decided to keep it.

Jesus asked, "Are all the keys here?"

Meyer replied, "All except one to a tiny closet in my heart."

Jesus said, "If you don't trust Me *in* all, don't trust me *at* all."

Sensing that Jesus was receding from him, Meyer finally offered the last key. Jesus took it, cleaned out the secret closet, and filled it with so much better.

"What a fool," Meyer thought of his reluctance, "Jesus wanted to take away fake jewels and give me real ones."

—Source unknown

Charles Finney's Seven Indications of Revival

1. When the sovereignty of God indicates that revival is near
2. When wickedness grieves and humbles Christians
3. When there is a spirit of prayer for revival
4. When the attention of ministers is directed toward revival
5. When Christians confess their sins one to another
6. When Christians are willing to make sacrifices to carry out the new movement of God's Spirit
7. When ministers and laity are willing for God to promote spiritual awakening by whatever instrument He pleases . . . then revival comes!

—Charles Finney

Failing to Take a Risk

One of the original group that helped launch the novel Apple computer, Ronald Wayne sold his 10 percent interest in the company for $800. Getting cold feet, and lacking a vision for Apple's future, he failed to take the initial investment risk and focus on the long-term dividend. That $800 investment would have later been worth more than $300 million.   —*Houston Chronicle*

Mountain-moving Members

The tiny congregation of a church in the Smokey Mountains received property from an estate. Days before dedicating the new church on the property, the building inspector advised that the parking lot was too small.

They used all of the property for the church construction, and the property was situated at the foothill of a mountain.

They called a prayer meeting that lasted several hours.

The next morning a contractor stopped by. "I'm building a shopping mall down the road," he explained. "And I am in desperate need of fill dirt."

The pastor pointed to the mountain, "We've got plenty of that!"

The contractor continued, "If you'll let me take the dirt from that mountain, I'll top off what's left and make you a parking lot."

Within a few weeks, the contractor had his fill dirt and the "mountain-moving members" had their parking lot.

—Larry and Kathy Miller[2]

"Whitsunday"

The feast of Pentecost came to be called "Whitsunday" in England. A logical reason (although it may not be historical) is that the term WHITSUNDAY is a contraction of WHITE SUNDAY. Because of the climate in England, the eve of Pentecost, rather than the eve of Easter became the time for baptisms (by immersion) because the weather is warmer then. The day was nicknamed for the white robes worn by the candidates for baptism.

—William Sydnor[3]

10

SPEAKER HELPS

Stan Toler Conference Favorites

(Note: In most cases, the original source and authors of the items listed are unknown. They have been e-mailed to me by friends like you.)

Top Ten Lists

Airline Announcements

10. Thank you for flying Delta Business Express. We hope you enjoyed giving us the business as much as we enjoyed taking you for a ride!
9. Your seat cushion can be used for flotation. In the event of an emergency water landing, please take the cushion—compliments of Reno Air.
8. Please use caution when opening the overhead bin. After a horrible landing like this you can be certain your luggage has shifted.
7. As you exit, please remember, there may be 50 ways to leave your lover, but there are only two ways out of this airplane!
6. After a high-speed landing in Phoenix, "WHOA, BIG FELLA', WHOA!"
5. Welcome aboard Southwest Airlines. In the event of a sudden loss of cabin pressure, oxygen masks will descend from the ceiling. Stop screaming and place it over your face.
4. Thanks for choosing TWA. We ask you to please remain seated as Captain Kangaroo bounces us to the terminal.
3. This is a nonsmoking flight. If you must smoke, please step out on the wing and watch our in-flight movie, *Gone with the Wind*.

2. Thank you for flying the friendly skies of United. Last one off the plane cleans it!

1. At American Airlines, we are pleased to have some of the best flight attendants in the industry. Unfortunately, none are on this flight.

Changes in the Church in the 21st Century

10. Work and Witness trips to Mars
9. Reclining pews
8. ATM machines during the offering
7. Scannable diapers for the nursery
6. Surround sound sermons
5. Computer chips in Bibles to locate them when lost or stolen
4. The all-in-one cup and wafer
3. Ministers of choreography
2. Drive-through worship
1. Copy machines that never break down

Innovative Ways to Make Baptism More Interesting

10. Add jelly fish.
9. Add a wave machine.
8. Make it a dunk tank and raise money for compassionate ministries.
7. Give a prize to whoever stays under the longest . . . and lives.
6. Beach balls!
5. Water slide.
4. Let the wet "baptisee" hug the dry saints.
3. Rubber duckies.
2. Jet Skis.
1. Bungee baptism!

Signs That It's Time to Join E-Mailers Anonymous

10. You write your screen name on a job application.
9. You surf without sunscreen.
8. You actually believe that something good will happen if you forward this message to seven more people.
7. Your devotions are e-mailed to you by ThyKing.com.

6. You get up in the middle of the night to go to the bathroom and check your e-mail.
5. You consider the "You've Got Mail" voice guy a father figure.
4. You spend half a flight with your laptop on your lap, and your child stored in the overhead bin.
3. The computer virus was harder on you than the flu.
2. You know all the AOL access numbers by heart.
1. After reading this list you forward it to everyone in your address book.

Things Overheard at the Pearly Gates

10. "No, they're not named after Bill Gates' mom!"
9. "Sorry, I never knew you!"
8. "I knew I shouldn't have ordered the meatloaf at Denny's."
7. "Could I see your supervisor?"
6. "I tried to tell 'em I was sick."
5. "But, I went to church at Christmas and Easter."
4. "If I'd-a known it was going to be this good, I would have eaten bacon instead of bran flakes."
3. "Listen, Pete, there could be a big tip in this for ya."
2. "This is a lot better than Indianapolis."
1. "Is that your final answer?"

Things Parishioners Do When the Sermon Is Boring

10. Crack their knuckles.
9. Eat a box of Tic-Tacs.
8. Clip their fingernails.
7. Clean out their purse.
6. Smile insincerely.
5. Slap their sleeping neighbor to see if he or she will turn the other cheek.
4. Make out grocery lists on the back of tithe envelopes.
3. Pass notes.
2. Play hangman.
1. Sleep!

Things People Won't Say When They See a Christian Bumper Sticker on Your Car

10. "Look! Let's stop that car and ask those folks how we can become Christians!"

9. "Don't worry, Billy. Those people are Christians—they must have a good reason why they're driving 90 miles per hour."

8. "What a joy to be sharing the highway with another car of Spirit-filled brothers and sisters."

7. "Isn't it wonderful how God blessed that Christian couple with a brand-new BMW?"

6. "Dad, how come people who drive like that don't get thrown in jail? Dad . . . can we get a bumper sticker like that, too?"

5. "Stay clear of those folks, Martha. If they get raptured, that car's gonna be all over the road."

4. "Oh, look! That Christian woman is getting a chance to share Jesus with a police officer."

3. "No, that's not garbage coming out of their windows, Bert—it's probably gospel tracts for the road workers."

2. "Oh, boy! We're in trouble now! We just rear-ended one of God's cars!"

1. "Quick, Alice, honk the horn, or they won't know that we love Jesus!"

Miscellaneous

Church Staff Job Descriptions

Senior Pastor
- Able to leap tall buildings in a single bound
- More powerful than a locomotive
- Faster than a speeding bullet
- Walks on water
- Makes policy with God

Executive Pastor
- Able to leap short buildings in a single bound
- As powerful as a switch engine
- Just as fast as a speeding bullet
- Walks on water if the sea is calm
- Talks with God

Minister of Music
- Leaps short buildings with a running start
- Almost as powerful as a switch engine
- Faster than a speeding BB
- Walks on water if he knows where the stumps are
- Is occasionally addressed by God

Minister of Youth
- Runs into small buildings
- Recognizes locomotives two out of three times
- Uses a squirt gun
- Knows how to use the water fountain
- Mumbles to himself

Church Secretary
- Lifts buildings to walk under them
- Kicks locomotives off the track
- Catches speeding bullets in her teeth
- Freezes water with a single glance
- When God speaks she says, "May I ask who is calling?"

Only in America . . .

. . . can a pizza get to your house faster than an ambulance.

. . . do drugstores make the sick walk all the way to the back of the store to get their prescriptions.

. . . do people order a double cheeseburger, a large order of fries, and a diet Coke.

. . . do banks leave both doors open and then chain the ballpoint pens to the counters.

. . . do we leave cars worth thousands of dollars in the driveway and leave useless junk in the garage.

. . . do we buy hot dogs in packages of ten and buns in packages of eight.

You Might Be a Preacher If . . .

. . . you've ever received an anonymous gift certificate from U-Haul.

. . . you've ever counted people at a sporting event.

. . . your office is "prayer-conditioned."

. . . you've ever wanted the soloist to sing on a hill far away.

. . . you've ever wanted to try multilevel tithing.

. . . running red lights in a funeral procession makes you feel important.

. . . you've ever wanted to a give the sound man a little feedback of your own.

. . . all your children have Bible names.

. . . you've ever seen an "In Memory Of" plate over a commode.

. . . you find negotiating with a terrorist easier than the church organist.

Funny Stories

Too Tired to Amen

A participant in one of my seminars wrote me a note thanking me for making the point that many Christian leaders are tired because they don't delegate enough duties to others. He said, "Stan, I wanted to shout 'Amen!' to that, but I was just too tired."

Willpower

A well-known panhandler approached a preacher who had been tipped off about the man's begging. As the preacher swept the walk in front of his church, the infamous panhandler approached him, "Are you Pastor Murphy?" "I am," said the preacher with a smile.

The man made his move, "Pastor, what would you say if I told you I haven't eaten in three days?" Quickly the pastor responded, "From the looks of you, I'd say you've got a lot of willpower!"

Pallbearers

A motivational speaker checked into the hotel room assigned by the welcoming committee for the event where he was speaking. When he took his routine security check underneath the king-size bed in his room he was startled to see a king-size dead cockroach.

The next morning he met his host for breakfast in the hotel's restaurant, the host asked him how the room was. A bit disgusted that his room wasn't exactly a five-star room, the speaker decided that honesty would be the best policy. "Well, sir, I guess I might as

well tell you that there was a giant cockroach lying under my bed."
The host just laughed it off, "Well, at least it was dead."

"You're right about that," the speaker said. "The dead cockroach didn't bother me, but his pallbearers kept me awake all night!"

Red Sea

The Vacation Bible School teacher had just finished the lesson about the crossing of the Red Sea. Way in the back row, a four-year-old with round glasses raised his hand and started waving. "Johnny, did you have a question?" "Sure, do," he said. "For the last hour you've been talking about the children of Israel walking into water over their heads. I'd just like to know where the grown-ups were when all this was goin' on?"

Lumberjack

A scrawny teenager applied for a job as a lumberjack. The supervisor tried not to laugh when he was asked about a job. "You . . . a lumberjack?" "Yes sir, I think I can handle the job," the boy replied. "I'll tell you what, you take this axe and go over yonder and cut that big ol' tree down."

"Yes, SIR!" the boy said. The axe was almost bigger than the teen, but about 15 minutes later, the supervisor went to check on him—and to his surprise, the tree was laying flat on the ground. "Boy, where in the world did you learn how to swing an axe like that?!" The scrawny teenager responded, "In the Sahara desert." The lumberman laughed out loud, "Boy, there aren't that many trees in the Sahara desert." "I know, Sir," the applicant said. "But you should have seen how many there were before I started cuttin' 'em down."

Honeymoon at the Beach

Strolling along the beach of a seaside resort the newlyweds were basking in the beauty of the waves crashing against the shore. Suddenly, the groom tried to wax eloquent, "Roll on, O beautiful ocean, back to where you came from; and leave me alone with my bride." The bride was awestruck to see the rolling of the waves—and awestruck that she just married the son of the richest man in town. She squeezed his arm and pointed to the ocean, "Look Harold! They're doing just what you told them to do!"

Air Conditioning

It was nearly a-hundred-degrees Fahrenheit inside the little church in West Virginia. The summer sing-along was just getting started when a visitor stood up and made his way back to the church's lone usher. He whispered, "Excuse me, it's a little stuffy in here. Would you be so kind as to turn down the air conditioner just a bit?" The usher stood tall in his new Harley Davidson T-shirt, "Not a problem." The man thanked him and made his way up the center aisle to sit with his wife, Gladys.

The sing-along was well into its sixth special by the ladies' trio from the Assemblies of God church, when the visitor stood up and made his way back up the aisle to the usher in the Harley David-son T-shirt. "Excuse me, my wife, Gladys, said she just about got a chill. Would you be so kind as to readjust the air conditioner?

Several trips up and down the aisle later, the ladies' trio ran out of accompaniment tracks, so the sing-along ended. As the visitor and his wife, Gladys, left the church he thanked the usher and headed out the door. The custodian went over to the usher and asked him what all that back and forth up the aisle stuff was all about. "He wanted to talk to me about the air conditioning. I just didn't have the heart to tell him we ain't got one."

Clean Restroom

A tour bus stopped in front of a convenience store that was a hundred miles from nowhere. Soon a lone passenger, a 60-year-old man on blood pressure medicine, descended the steps of the bus and walked hurriedly to the side of the store, where there was a door with a sign made out of an old license plate. Scribbled on the plate with a magic marker was the word "MEN." The man on blood pressure medicine tried to open the door but it was locked.

He hurried back to the front door of the convenience store and said to the woman at the counter, "Got a key to the restroom?" "Yep," she said, after she had taken a sip from a 64-ounce cup of soda. "Well, could I borrow it?" the man said sarcastically. The attendant pointed to the wall near the door. There was the key, tied with some twisted wire to a beaten-up Chevy hubcap.

The man grabbed the hubcap with the key and walked out the door—past the tour bus, back to the restroom. Soon he made the return trip back to the counter—past the tour bus—back to the attendant. "I know why you locked that bathroom door," the man said with disgust. The attendant took another sip from the 64-ounce cup and said, "Why's that?" As the man handed her the hubcap he said, loud enough for everyone on the tour bus to hear, "BECAUSE SOMEONE MIGHT SNEAK IN THERE AND CLEAN IT!"

Oversell

Once I was trying to build an effective introduction to a sermon on the story of the Ethiopian eunuch. The audience was with me, until I strayed from the text to emphasize a point.

"This Ethiopian eunuch was a splendid man of character. He was a servant of the court; he was trusted by the queen; and he was even treasurer of the court."

The next line put some puzzled looks on the audience faces. "And no doubt, the Ethiopian eunuch was a good husband and father to his family . . ."[1]

Hit 'im Again!

A church was having a problem meeting its budget. The pastor suggested to the board that a special fund be established to meet the crisis. During the discussion, the pastor recommended that the leaders set an example by being the first to contribute to the emergency budget fund.

As he made the suggestion, he looked straight into the eyes of a board member who was "well-to-do." The problem was, the board member was known only to be a man of means but also to be one of the community's stingiest men. Feeling the obligation of the pastor's call to make a financial commitment, the board member finally spoke up, "Preacher, I'll give $25."

Just then, a small piece of plaster fell from the ceiling and hit the board member on the head. "I'll make that $50!" he quickly declared. The church treasurer was heard to pray, "Hit ' im again, Lord, hit 'im again!"[2]

The New Congressman

A newly elected congressman, who thought a little more highly of himself than he should have, went to his new office on Capitol Hill. The only things in his office were a chair, a desk, and a telephone.

He sat down in his bug burgundy leather executive chair. Into his office came a man who appeared to be a news reporter. The freshman congressman thought he'd better pick up the phone and act important. So he carried on a fictitious conversation, "Yes, Mr. President, I'm doing well—the office is great! How's the family? No, I'm sorry, I can't make it for dinner tonight—I'm working on a very important piece of legislation. Perhaps another time. Best to you, too, sir!"

He hung up the phone and said, "So are you with MSNBC? CNN?"

The man replied, "No, I'm with AT&T, and I'm here to hook up your phone."[3]

That's Living!

A man was extremely proud of the things he owned. But his most prized possession was his car, a brand-new Lexus. Loaded with more options than a menu in a Chinese restaurant, the automobile was the envy of his friends (and a couple of relatives). The car had become the central thing in his life. In fact, he put a clause in his will that in the event of his death, he would be buried in that car—probably making it quite difficult to line up any pallbearers.

The dreaded day arrived, and his last wishes were carried out.

At the cemetery, one of his envious friends watched as his buddy was lowered in the grave, car and all, and he was overcome with emotion. "Man," he exclaimed, "that's really living!"[4]

Discovery of America

A history professor commented on Christopher Columbus's discovery of America, saying that there were three significant aspects of the trip. One, before he left, he didn't have a clue as to where he was going. Two, when he arrived, he didn't have a clue as to where he was. And, three, when he got ready to leave, he didn't have a clue as to how to get back home.[5]

Hog Caller

A middle-aged preacher had just taken a new church in another state. Once he was settled in, he decided to join a local civic organization. The organization's president was happy to greet the minister, but she told the minister that she had some bad news.

"We only take one person from each vocation in our group, Reverend." She said, "And we already have a minister. As a matter of fact, every vocation in this community is represented in our group right now, with the exception of a hog caller. She embarrassingly asked the next question, "Would you mind being a hog caller among us?"

"Well," said the pastor, "where I come from I'm considered a 'shepherd,' but I suppose you know your people better than I do."[6]

Lemonade Stand

A nine-year-old set up a lemonade stand in front of his house. An economist was driving by and spotted the hand-lettered cardboard sign on the front of the stand that read, "Lemonade $5." The economist stopped the car and got out to talk to the young entrepreneur, "Son, even with inflation, that's quite a high price for lemonade."

The nine-year-old quicky replied, "Mister, buy the lemonade if you want to, but please don't tell me how to run a business!"[7]

They Both Jumped

A fellow was about ready to jump from a bridge. An alert police officer slowly, methodically moved toward him, talking with him all the time.

When he got within inches of the man, he said, "Surely nothing could be bad enough for you to take your life. Tell me about it. Talk to me."

The would-be jumper told how his wife had left him, how his business had become bankrupt, how his friends had deserted him. Everything in life had lost meaning.

For 30 minutes he told the sad story. Then they *both* jumped![8]

Afraid of the Dark

A little girl was afraid to go to bed in the dark by herself. After three or four trips to her parents' bedroom, her father sought to reassure her, "Look, honey," he said, "you are not really alone in your bedroom. God is watching over you. God is everywhere, and He is in your bedroom."

The little girl was not reassured. She started back to her room but stopped at the door and said in a loud whisper, "God, if You're in there, please don't say anything. It would scare me to death."[9]

Soccer Mom

A soccer mom was driving the team home from a winning game. The junior athletes packed the minivan and they were boisterous to say the least. Distracted by the noise coming from the back of the van, Mom didn't see the stop sign.

Soon the car with the revolving blue light came into view in the side mirror. Standing by the opened window, the policeman looked at the vanload of kids in the back and then at the driver. As he pulled out his notebook he looked to the frustrated driver and said, "Looks like you didn't know when to stop."

The soccer mom shot back, "And what make you think all these belong to me?"[10]

Trapped in a New Car

My first new car was a 1968 Volkswagen Beetle. It had a lot of neat gadgets, including an eight-track tape player hidden in the glove compartment. It also had seat belts, which had recently become a requirement of the law.

One day I asked my friend Kenny Bullock to join me for a ride in my shiny green VW. We drove to see a couple of girls on the west side of town.

We pulled in front of their house and, like any nervous 17-year-olds, fervently planned our strategy to impress the girls. We mustered the courage to go to the door and ask them out for a ride in my new car.

But we were trapped!

We had both fastened our seat belts, and we couldn't find the release button! Frantically we read the manual, searched the seats, and even asked a passing stranger, all to no avail.

Just about that time the girls came out of the house and noticed us sitting at the curb. With a grin, they came over to the car and asked what we were doing in the neighborhood.

I've often wondered how long they had stood at the front window and watched us sitting like two idiots, wondering if we were ever going to get out of the car.

We covered our embarrassment by acting as if everything was perfectly fine. We even asked if they wanted a ride in the new car. Their ready acceptance left us scrambling for a reply. Spying the gas gauge, I told them that we'd go get some gas and come right back.

We drove straight to the nearest gas station, where we bought 50 cents worth of gas and asked the attendant to free us from the seat belts. Laughing loudly, he reached behind the seats to a well-hidden release button. Finally we were free![11]

Horseback Riding

A lady concerned about her friend's overweight condition invited her to go horseback riding for some exercise. Reluctantly the friend agreed and, with some effort, finally slithered and squirmed into an old pair of jeans. With a little help, she also put on a pair of cowboy boots. After the whole dressing ordeal, the friend said to the new cowgirl, "You look great!"

"I don't feel great," she answered.

"Why's that?" her friend inquired.

"I was just thinking about that horse. He thinks he's going jogging, but it'll be more like weight lifting."[12]

AUTHOR INFORMATION

Dr. Stan Toler
P.O. Box 892170
Oklahoma City, OK 73189-2170

E-mail: stoler1107@aol.com

For a complete listing of books and other resources by Stan Toler,
visit his Web site:
www.stantoler.com

NOTES

Front Matter

    1. *Wikipedia*, s.v. "Public Speaking," http://en.wikipedia.org/wiki/Public_speaking

Introduction

    1. Charlie Jones, "A Sense of Urgency," My Article Archive, http://www.myarticlearchive.com/articles/7/206.htm

    2. Timothy J. Koegel, *The Exceptional Presenter* (Austin, Tex.: Greenleaf Book Group Press, 2007), 20.

Chapter 1

    1. Source unknown. Adapted by author.

    2. Quoteland.com, http://www.quoteland.com/author.asp?AUTHOR_ID=352.

    3. http://www.elise.com/web/a/public_speaking_tips.php

    4. http://www.aresearchguide.com/3tips.html

    5. http://www.unausa.org/site/pp.asp?c=fvKRI8MPJpF&b=457149

    6. http://www.famous-speeches-and-speech-topics.info/giving-writing-speeches/g10-gestures.htm

Chapter 2

    1. Mark Sanborn, "Seven Reasons Why Speakers Flop," http://www.maximumimpact.com/articles/read/article_7_reasons_why_speakers_flop/

    2. Zig Ziglar, http://www.brainyquote.com/quotes/authors/z/zig_ziglar.html

    3. http://www.mindtools.com/CommSkll/PublicSpeaking.htm

    4. Haddon W. Robinson, quoted in Mark Galli and Craig Brian Larson, *Preaching That Connects* (Grand Rapids: Zondervan, 1994), 9.

    5. James O. Davis, "32 Quotes on Effective Preaching," http://www.sermoncentral.com/article.asp?article=a-James_Davis_12_31_07&ac=true

    6. http://www.famous-speeches-and-speech-topics.info/giving-writing-speeches/g14-speed-of-delivery.htm

Chapter 3

    1. Michael Heath, "PANIC," http://www.mhconsult.com/talkingbusiness_0804.html

    2. Koegel, *Exceptional Presenter*, 42.

    3. Sanborn, "Seven Reasons Why Speakers Flop."

Chapter 4

    1. Galli and Larson, *Preaching That Connects*, 26.

    2. Stan Toler, *Stan Toler's Practical Guide to Pastoral Ministry* (Indianapolis: Wesleyan Publishing House, 2007), 279-80.

    3. http://www.public-speaking.org/public-speaking-props-article.htm

    4. Henry O. Dormann, *The Speaker's Book of Quotations* (New York: Fawcett Columbine, 1987), 202.

5. Ed Stetzer, "Contextualized Preaching," http://www.sermoncentral.com/articleb.asp?article=PreachingPledge2

6. http://www.publicspeakingtip.org/speaking-qualities/illustrations.php

7. http://www.actnow.com.au/Tool/Tips_on_public_speaking.aspx

8. http://www.preachingtoday.com/skills/consideringhearers/200404.24.html?start=2

Chapter 5

1. Dormann, *Speaker's Book of Quotations,* 201.

2. Joseph Addison, quoted in *Write Better, Speak Better: How Words Can Work Wonders for You* (Pleasantville, N.Y.: Readers Digest Association, 1972), 385.

3. http://www.stresscure.com/jobstress/speak.html

4. http://www.ljlseminars.com/remember.htm

Chapter 7

1. http://www.preaching.com/resources/preacher_to_preacher/11546984/

Chapter 8

1. Quoted in Charles L. Wallis, ed., *Speaker's Illustrations for Special Days* (Grand Rapids: Baker Book House, 1956).

2. Ibid.

3. *Daylight Devotional Bible* (Grand Rapids: Zondervan Corporation, 1988), 1263.

4. Chuck Colson, "Opinion," *Moody Monthly* (May 1987).

5. Mark Connolly, "Advent," http://www.spirituality.org/issue04/page 11.html (9/27/99)

6. *Improving Your Serve* (Waco, Tex.: Word Books, 1981), 112-13.

7. Charles Foster, *Focus on the Family Magazine,* http://www.sermons.org/illustrations.html

8. Eleanor Doan, comp., *The Speaker's Sourcebook* (Grand Rapids: Zondervan, 1960).

9. Bob Phillips, ed., *The World's All-Time Best Collection of Good Clean Jokes* (New York: Galahad Books, 1996).

10. Lowell D. Streiker, comp., *An Encyclopedia of Humor* (Peabody, Mass.: Hendrickson Publishers, 1998).

11. Quoted in King Duncan, *Dynamic Illustrations* (Knoxville, Tenn.: Seven Worlds Publishing, 1996).

12. *The Grace Awakening* (Nashville: Word, 1996).

13. http://www.biblestudytools.net/SermonHelps/AutoIllustrator/index

14. http://www.sermonillustrations.com/a-z/b/baptism.htm

15. *Illustrating Great Words of the New Testament* (Nashville: Broadman Press, 1991).

16. *The Speaker's Quote Book* (Grand Rapids: Kregel, 1997).

17. Quoted in Frank S. Mead, comp., *12,000 Religious Quotations* (Grand Rapids: Baker Book House, 1989).

18. Quoted in ibid.

19. *Pulpit Preaching,* quoted in Mead, *12,000 Religious Quotations.*

20. Dennis J. Hester, comp., *The Vance Havner Quote Book* (Grand Rapids: Baker Book House, 1986), 13.

21. Ibid.

22. Ibid.

23. www.howstuffworks.com

24. *Guidepost*, 1978, quoted in *Pastor's Worship Resource* (Kansas City: Beacon Hill Press of Kansas City, 1987).

25. Mead, *12,000 Religious Quotations*, 70.

26. *Knight's Master Book of New Illustrations* (Grand Rapids: Eerdmans Publishing, 1956), 78.

27. http://www.hiaspire.com/newyear/stories.htm

28. Doan, *Speaker's Sourcebook*, 58.

29. "The Head Man," *Bluebook* (Dec. 1955).

30. Quoted in Hester, *Vance Havner Quote Book*.

31. *The Greatest Moments* (Nashville: Countryman, 1995), 20.

32. *Be a People Person* (Wheaton, Ill.: Victor Books, 1989), 145.

33. "Faithfulness Without Fanfare," *Decision* (February 1994), 11.

34. "Illustrations for Preaching," *The Clergy Journal* (September 1983).

35. Quoted in Michael P. Green, ed., *Illustrations for Biblical Preaching* (Grand Rapids: Baker Book House, 1989).

36. Quoted in Edward K. Rowell, ed., *Humor for Preaching and Teaching* (Grand Rapids: Baker Books, 1996).

37. "How Not to Celebrate Communion," *The Preacher's Magazine* (June/July/August 1996), 22.

38. "Let Us Celebrate Communion," *The Preacher's Magazine* (October 1977), 15.

39. *Vision of a World Hungry* (Nashville: Upper Room, 1979).

40. *Fully Alive* (St. Meinrad: Abbey Press, 1976).

41. *Developing a Giving Church* (Kansas City: Beacon Hill Press of Kansas City, 1999).

42. Quoted in Samuel Ward Hutton, *A Minister's Manual* (Grand Rapids: Baker Book House, 1958).

43. *Amusing Grace* (Knoxville, Tenn.: Seven Worlds Corporation, 1993).

44. Ibid.

45. *Dynamic Preaching*, Vol. X, No. 4 (April 1995).

46. Quoted in Duncan and Akers, *Amusing Grace*.

47. Quoted in James Hewett, comp., *Illustrations Unlimited* (Wheaton, Ill.: Tyndale House, 1988).

48. "Reflections on the Psalms," chap. 5, quotes in *Pastor's Weekly Briefing*, Vol. 6, No. 15 (April 10, 1998).

49. Quoted in *Illustrations Unlimited* (Wheaton, Ill.: Tyndale House, 1988).

50. Ibid.

51. Ibid.

52. Quoted in Cal Samra and Rose Samra, *Holy Humor: Inspirational Wit and Cartoons* (New York: Master Media Limited, 1996).

53. Quoted in Albert Wells Jr., ed., *Inspiring Quotations* (Nashville: Thomas Nelson, 1988).

54. Quoted in *Dynamic Preaching*, Vol. X, No. 4 (April 1995).
55. Quoted in Hewett, *Illustrations Unlimited*.
56. Ibid.
57. Ibid.
58. Quoted in Wells, *Inspiring Quotations*.
59. Samra and Samra, *Holy Humor*.
60. Quoted in Green, *Illustrations for Biblical Preaching*.
61. *Reader's Digest* (June 1996), 103.
62. Paul Lee Tan, ed., *Resource* (March/April 1991).
63. Max Lucado, *In the Eye of the Storm* (Nashville: Word, 1991).
64. *Hot Illustrations for Youth Talks* (El Cajon, Calif.: Youth Specialties, 1994).
65. Quoted in Wells, *Inspiring Quotations*.
66. Ibid.
67. Ibid.
68. *Houston Chronicle* (October 29, 1999), 2B.
69. "Valley of Death's Shadow," *Preaching Today*, Tape 131.
70. Quoted in Green, *Illustrations for Biblical Preaching*.
71. Ibid.
72. "Valley of Death's Shadow," *Preaching Today*, Tape 131.
73. Max Lucado, *A Gentle Thunder* (Nashville: Word, 1995).
74. *In the Eye of the Storm*.
75. Quoted in Duncan, *Dynamic Illustrations*.
76. Quoted in John K. Bergland, *Abingdon Preacher's Annual 1994* (Nashville: Abingdon Press, 1994).
77. Quoted in Green, *Illustrations For Biblical Preaching*.
78. "Bruno," *Herald of Holiness* (March 1997), 47.
79. Quoted in Duncan, *Dynamic Illustrations*.
80. *Perfect Love* (North Attleboro, Mass.: J. A. Wood, 1884), 96.
81. "Entire Sanctification," Christian Classics Ethereal Library, http://www.ccel.org/ccel/clarke/entire_sanct.iii.html.
82. Ibid.
83. *The Pursuit of God* (Treasures Media Inc., 2007), 19.
84. *God's Best Secrets* (Grand Rapids: Kregel Publications, 1994), 34.
85. *Revival Fire* (Grand Rapids: Zondervan, 1995), 12.
86. Quoted in Josiah H. Gilbert, *Three Thousand Selected Quotations from Brilliant Writers* (1909), 545.
87. Cal Samra and Rose Samra, "What Is the Name of Our Country?" in *More Holy Humor* (Nashville: Thomas Nelson Publishers, 1997).
88. Quoted in Duncan, *Dynamic Illustrations*.
89. Ibid.
90. Quoted in *America's God and Country Encyclopedia of Quotations* (Dallas: Fame Publishing, Inc., 1996).
91. Quoted in ibid.
92. Ibid.
93. Quoted in *The Pastor's Weekly Briefing*, Vol. 6, No. 27 (July 3, 1998).
94. Quoted in Dick DeVos, *Rediscovering American Values: The Foundations of Our Freedom for the 21st Century* (New York: Plume Printing, 1997).

95. Samra and Samra, *More Holy Humor*.

96. Quoted in Wallis, *Speaker's Illustrations for Special Days*.

97. "The Ultimate Home Security System," quoted in Michael Duduit, ed., *The Abingdon Preaching Annual 1967* (Nashville: Abingdon Press, 1996).

98. Doan, *Speaker's Sourcebook*.

99. Quoted in Carroll E. Simcox, ed., *Four Thousand Four Hundred Quotations for Christian Communicators* (Grand Rapids: Baker Book House, 1991).

100. Duncan and Akers, *Amusing Grace*.

101. Doan, *Changing Times, Speaker's Sourcebook*.

102. Ibid.

103. Quoted in Duncan, *Dynamic Illustrations*.

104. Ibid.

105. Quoted in Streiker, *Encyclopedia of Humor*.

106. Quoted in Duncan, *Dynamic Illustrations*.

107. "King's Biography" (October 4, 1999), http://stanford.edu/group/King/Biography/briefbio.htm

108. Quoted in *The African-American Devotional Bible* (Grand Rapids: Zondervan Publishing House, 1997).

109. Quoted in Green, *Illustrations for Biblical Preaching*.

110. Duncan and Akers, *Amusing Grace*.

111. Ibid.

112. Rewritten from Annie's Homepage: http://www.annieshomepage.com/motherday.htm

113. The Pastor's Story File (May 1998), submitted by Teresa Yates.

114. *The Essential Calvin & Hobbes*, quoted in Duncan and Akers, *Amusing Grace*, 130.

115. Quoted in Michael Duduit, *Abingdon Preaching Annual 1998*.

116. *Macartney's Illustrations* (New York: Abingdon Press, 1955).

117. *Living Faith* (New York: Random House, Inc., 1996), 58.

118. "The Grandmother of Us All," Christianity Today, http://www.christianity.net/ct/6TA/6TA044.html

119. Duncan and Akers, *Amusing Grace*.

120. Ibid.

121. Quoted in Wells, *Inspiring Quotations*.

122. Robert R. Kopp, "Mother's Day/Father's Day," quoted in Duduit, *Abingdon Preaching Annual 1966*.

123. http://skali.com.my/microsites/skali/events/mday/mday6.html

124. *Saturday Evening Post* (May/June 1999), 68.

125. Duncan and Akers, *Amusing Grace*.

126. Quoted in G. B. F. Hallock, Richard R. Smith, *Five Thousand Best Modern Illustrations* (New York: George H. Doran Co., 1927).

127. Ibid.

128. Ibid.

129. Ibid.

130. Quoted in Wells, *Inspiring Quotations*.

131. Ibid.

132. Ibid.

133. "The Sacredness of Human Life," http://www.erle.com/Sundays/1997/Sermons/97s-sanctity.htm

134. Ibid.

135. Quoted in Duncan, *Dynamic Illustrations.*

136. Quoted in ibid.

137. Quoted in Stan Toler, *Stewardship Starters* (Kansas City: Beacon Hill Press of Kansas City, 1996).

138. "Growing Generous Givers," http://www.christianity.net/leadership/8L3/8L3090.html

139. Quoted in Stan Toler and Elmer Towns, *Developing a Giving Church* (Kansas City: Beacon Hill Press of Kansas City, 1999).

140. Quoted in Jim Burns and Greg McKinnon, *Illustrations, Stories, and Quotes to Hang Your Message On* (Ventura, Calif.: Gospel Light, 1997).

141. Quoted in *The Evangel.*

142. Quoted in Duncan, *Dynamic Illustrations.*

143. "Growing Generous Givers," http://www.christianity.net/leadership/8L3/8L3090.html

144. Quoted in Toler, *Stewardship Starters.*

145. Quoted in ibid.

146. Ibid.

147. *Walking with Christ in the Details of Life* (Nashville: Thomas Nelson Publishers, 1992), 40.

148. Quoted in Toler, *Stewardship Starters.*

149. Quoted in ibid.

150. "Quotes & Comments," *The United Church Observer* (Sept. 1996), 55.

151. Quoted in Duncan and Akers, *Amusing Grace.*

152. "What Have I Thanked God for Today?" *Christian Reader* (July/August 1998).

153. Quoted in Wallis, *Speaker's Illustrations for Special Days.*

154. Quoted in Yvonne Zipp, "Gratitude and Giving in the 1990s," http://www.csmonitor.com/durable/1998/1/25/fp1-csm.shtml

155. Quoted in Wallis, ed., *Speaker's Illustrations for Special Days.*

156. Found on the Internet.

157. Paul Lee Tan, ed., *Resource* (January/February 1991).

158. *The Family Circus,* King Features Syndicate.

159. http://people.howstuffworks.com/18-tips-for-public-speaking2.htm

160. http://www.aresearchguide.com/3tips.html

Chapter 9

1. *The Christian Index* (Jan. 28, 1999), 10.

2. *God's Vitamin C for the Spirit* (Lancaster, Pa.: Starburst Publishers, 1996), 55.

3. *More than Words* (New York: Harper & Row, 1990).

Chapter 10

1. Stan Toler and Martha Bolton, *That Ain't Just Preaching: A View from Pew* (Cleveland: Pathway Press, 2005), 51.

2. Toler and Towns, *Developing a Giving Church,* 30.

3. Stan Toler, *The Buzzards Are Circling, but God's Not Finished with Me Yet* (Tulsa: RiverOak Publishing, 2001), 39-40

4. Stan Toler, *God Is Never Late, He's Seldom Early, He's Always on Time* (Kansas City: Beacon Hill Press of Kansas City, 2004), 83.

5. Stan Toler and Jerry Brecheisen, *Lead to Succeed: New Testament Principles for Visionary Leadership* (Kansas City: Beacon Hill Press of Kansas City, 2003), 11.

6. Stan Toler and Jerry Brecheisen, *Maximum Integrity: Leadership Insights from the Psalms* (Kansas City: Beacon Hill Press of Kansas City, 2006), 42-43.

7. Stan Toler, Terry Toler, and Mark Hollingsworth, *He Still Speaks* (Kansas City: Beacon Hill Press of Kansas City, 2008), 48.

8. Stan Toler, *God Has Never Failed Me, but He Sure Has Scared Me to Death a Few Times* (Tulsa: Honor Books, 1995), 45-46.

9. Ibid., 84.

10. Stan Toler and Debra White Smith, *The Harder I Laugh, the Deeper I Hurt* (Kansas City: Beacon Hill Press of Kansas City, 2001), 21.

11. Ibid., 127-28.

12. Stan Toler, *Minute Motivators for Dieters* (Tulsa: RiverOak Publishing, 2002), 129.